CU00929241

About the Author

The Author was educated at the prestigious Vine Comprehensive School in Basingstoke, from where he went to college. He then moved on to work on various building sites, which paid for him to go surfing in California in the early eighties.

Upon his return, he procured various jobs in construction, including hod-carrying, roof-tiling and property renovation. He is not sure how, but he then managed to find gainful employment as an International Reinsurance Broker at Lloyds of London.

To cut a long story short, he left the rat race in the late 90s and gained a degree in English Law with Spanish Law and has since pursued some charitable endeavours. One such venture led to him writing this unique insight into life in the Peruvian Andes, where all is not what it appears to be.

Dedication

For Vilma and her friends. With thanks.

Philip J.S. Jones

A PERUVIAN DIARY

AUSTIN MACAULEY PUBLISHERS™
LONDON • CAMBRIDGE • NEW YORK • SHARJAH

A CIP catalogue record for this title is available from the British Library.

ISBN 978-1-78693-862-6 (Paperback)
ISBN 978-1-78693-863-3 (Hardback)
ISBN 978-1-78693-864-0 (E-Book)
www.austinmacauley.com

First Published (2017)
Austin Macauley Publishers™ Ltd.
25 Canada Square
Canary Wharf
London
E14 5LQ

Acknowledgments

The author would like to thank all of those people who helped in the production of this book.

Especially those who taught him so much about life and love and happiness in the highlands of the Andes, without whom this book would not have been possible, and about whom this book has been written.

A True Story

I flew to Peru in September 2009 expecting to assist in the building of a soup kitchen in a shanty town in Lima, on behalf of a charity; but that did not come to fruition. I found myself instead, living in a small village, building a children's dormitory, at 3,700m high in the Andes. A place where I discovered what I think was the origin of the legend of El Dorado, the fabled city of gold, and much more besides.

This is a diary of my adventures in the Peruvian Andes, living and working alongside the local people.

All the names have been changed to protect those involved.

The Author

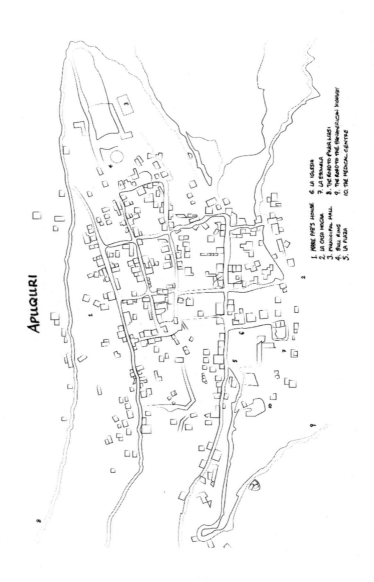

APUQURI

1. MIKE PAPI'S HOUSE
2. LA CASA HOGAR
3. MUNICIPAL HALL
4. BULL RING
5. LA PLAZA
6. LA IGLESIA
7. LA ESCUELA
8. THE ROAD TO PUKA WASI
9. THE ROAD TO THE PANAMERICAN HIGHWAY
10. THE MEDICAL CENTRE

SOUTH AMERICA

PANAMA

VENEZUELA

GUYANA

French Guiana

COLOMBIA

Suriname

ECUADOR

BRAZIL

PERU

BOLIVIA

APUQURI

PARAGUAY

CHILE

URUGUAY

ARGENTINA
(1853)

GB (1833)

By the same Author

The Story of Chuletas

One man… One lamb… One true story.

A delightful tale of the author's efforts to hand rear his four day old orphaned lamb, in a University apartment block in Northern Spain.

The Story of Chuletas gets under the skin of Spanish culture with some surprising results.

The Flight of the Condor

Legend has it that many years ago, high in the mountains of the Andes, a condor soared high above a small village, and in that village there lived a young woman who was very beautiful. The condor flew over the village many times and was so drawn to the young woman that one night he dropped down from the sky into the village and took the form of a young man. His suit was black and his collar white, his shoes were a deep dark red, but he could not change completely.

He went to the young woman's house in the still of the night and knocked on her door. Being impressed by his appearance and being of a generous nature, the young woman invited him in for something to eat; the only light coming from the fire in the kitchen upon which she warmed the food. She did not notice that his hands were feathers hidden inside his suit, and that he could only eat with his beak from the bowl, which he did, when she looked away.

He became rapidly enamoured with the young woman and came to visit her again, several times in fact, when they would talk well into the night. Until one evening, the bowl slipped, the light flickered and she saw his hands; terrified, she held her composure and acted as though nothing had happened. She kept talking until the sun began to rise. As the sunlight fell upon the day, his suit began to change, he began to revert to his original form, and in fear she ran away.

The condor never forgot that young woman, but he knew that he could never return to see her ever again. And the young woman knew that she would never invite a stranger into her house ever again; because all is not what it appears to be.

A Peruvian Diary

Tuesday 1st September

I took a nine hour flight at 9.00 a.m. from London Gatwick to Atlanta, Georgia, USA, where there was a four hour wait for my connection to the six hour flight to Lima Peru, that's a lot of hours if you think about it. Even though I'd been to Lima the previous year I was slightly apprehensive; though I have always found the fearful rumours of danger in South America to be vastly exaggerated, a seed of doubt remained. A middle aged European could appear to the unscrupulous South American as quite a rich target in a developing country such as Peru. Despite any trepidation within me, I was relieved to touch down at Lima, after all if man were supposed to fly he would have been given wings, that is, apart from those of a Boeing 757 (there are other aircraft).

Lima is a fabulously large city, founded on 15 January 1535 as the Ciudad de Los Reyes (City of the Kings) by the Spanish explorer Francisco Pizarro. It flourished as the commercial centre of the Spanish Empire from the mid-1500's until several earthquakes destroyed much of the city in 1687. This natural disaster allowed other cities such as Buenos Aires to take over the mantle as the continent's leaders in international trade. Until that time all commerce within the Spanish South American Empire was required to pass through the port of Lima and where tribute was paid to the authorities, which is what made Lima the wealthiest city in all of South America at the time; the city was for some time the central trading link between the Far East, the Spanish Americas and Europe.

Much later, following some decline, Lima was significant as the meeting point of the two great liberators of Spanish South America, on 22 July 1822.

Simon Bolivar had begun his campaign of liberation of the Northern States of the Southern Continent in 1813 as a general of the former New Granada, now known as Colombia. During eight years Bolivar succeeded in the separation of Colombia, Venezuela, Panama, and Ecuador from empirical Spanish rule, he finally liberated Bolivia, which was made a Republic on 6ᵗʰ August 1825.

In the south of the continent, following the independence of Argentina, the Argentinean General Jose de San Martin travelled across the Andes to liberate Chile from Spain in 1818. He later set sail from Chile to attack Lima which he occupied on 21 July 1821; the independence of Peru from Spain was declared just one week later on 28 July 1821. San Martin was then elected by democratic vote as "Protector" of the newly independent nation. In his honour, the most attractive square in the centre of Lima is named La Plaza de San Martin.

Though the majority of the colonial buildings are somewhat rundown these days, much of Lima's Spanish colonial past is evident today in the centre of the city. It is not difficult to imagine the former grandeur that Lima held as a centre of world trade.

Sadly over the years, the city has become an incredibly dusty sprawl of low rise buildings that spread out from the urban centre. The population swelled to around 9,000,000 in the 1980's at a time when many campesinos (members of the rural peasant classes) moved into the city to escape the violent threat of the Sendero Luminoso (Shining Path) terrorist movement. The immigrant campesinos have built impoverished shanty towns in the desert like periphery of the city; these barrios are fully occupied and still expanding. The majority of the populous moved from the far away isolation of the mountainous regions of bucolic Peru, to begin an entirely different city life. They had lived in what some would say was a primitive way; they had lived a simple rural life, very much aligned with nature. So separated were the customs of the campesinos that, when they first moved to Lima, they were known to have the habit of squatting in the street to relieve themselves in broad daylight.

* * *

I took my bags through the nothing to declare channel at around 11.00 p.m. local time. It was a smooth easy entry into the country; where clearly the authorities welcome foreign tourism. You are not a potential terrorist as a European, you are not someone who may cause unspeakable atrocities with a toothpick or a tub of face cream at any moment without warning; you are, in fact, a welcome source of foreign income. Peru is a friendly country, the authorities like their own people so much that if they can afford to go abroad, they have to leave a financial deposit, to be returned upon their return, as an incentive to return. The Peruvian authorities, quite simply, like to have people around. This may be because the population of this enormous country is relatively sparse, at just under 30,000,000; and almost a third of them live in Lima.

After having passed through customs, I found a warm, still, comfortable evening and it was around about 11.30 p.m. by the time I met Carolina, the head of the orphanage I was to visit. She was a large woman with a big, charming, personality to match; she had the dark, brown skinned complexion of most Peruvians, her high cheekbones gave some credence to her friendly welcoming face, she had a huge vivacious smile, I liked her almost before I had met her.

We went outside into the glow of the evening to a waiting taxi, a rough old blue Japanese estate car. As the taxi swerved through vibrant streets in the centre of town towards the dodgem track that is the freeway to the south of the city, Carolina told me that the orphanage which I was about to visit, had been built about eight years previously, on the site of what had been an ancient Inca cemetery. When the footings had been excavated, they had discovered several ancient Inca tombs, which were promptly declared to the authorities. At the time the powers that be had no interest in the archaeology of the place. So in their infinite wisdom, the builders had put the old invaluable urns and vases on the skip and they had been obliterated, in effect the artefacts in the tombs had been sent to the tip. I found such pointless destruction quite disturbing and Carolina didn't seem too pleased either, nonetheless she was almost matter of fact in her way; this had all happened long before she had begun working at the project, and what could be done now? Not a lot it seemed, which brought a tear to my eye. Those artefacts, if sold, could have funded the orphanage for years.

The orphanage cared for around thirty youngsters, aged between 5 and 16 years, who were mostly from broken homes; normally the father had disappeared and left the mother to fend alone with several children. There are no social services to speak of in Peru; this makes an incredibly difficult situation one that is virtually impossible to manage. Without help a mother may need to send her children to live in another place, or they might not eat at all.

At around 12.30 a.m., after an hour or so in the taxi, we pulled up off the freeway into a warm sandy street, at the steel gate of the rather incongruous white stonewalled orphanage in the arid, shanty town of North Comas District. It was unfortunate that I was asked to pay a vastly inflated taxi fare of 80 sols (£16.00); it left a slightly bitter taste in the mouth, not for the money, but for the principle. I later learned that the fare should have been at most Sol. 20 someone was making a considerable profit, and it wasn't the driver.

As we got out of the cab there were a few people wandering in the dimly lit, sand covered streets, accompanied of course by the inimitable dogs that run free as they often seem to do in South America. We rang the bell at the reinforced, steel-doored entrance to the compound and after a short minute or so, the tannoy buzzed us in, amidst a brief flurry of Spanish, the door was opened for us, by a sweet petite Peruvian woman, Marta.

The orphanage was built in an area the approximate size of two earthen grey football pitches devoid of any grass. Within the walls there were basically three main structures; an imposing pair of relatively recent whitewashed two story buildings and the original low slung flat-roofed building of single story dormitories, with adjoining communal bathrooms, a large dining area and kitchen built alongside; all painted in pink, yellow and a deep red in the occasionally colourful, South American way. Behind that was a ramshackle garden that had a seating area beneath a pagoda type framework in the centre, and adjacent to that was the caretaker's whitewashed, concrete breezeblock workshop in a far corner.

I was shown around a little, but it was late so I was taken to my rather functional stark, whitewashed room, on the top floor of one of the new rectangular buildings. From my room I could see out across to the distant hills that led down to the sea on the unseen side. The faraway lights of the shanty towns flickered on the surrounding hills, through the haze of the polluted city. As I sat in the echoing silence of the night, I had a couple of shots of the Grants duty-free that I had picked up in Atlanta. Whisky can have its uses when you find yourself far away in a developing country. It was around 1.00 a.m. by the time I finally got to sleep.

Wednesday 2ⁿᵈ September

After only a few hours' sleep, I woke up at around 6.00 a.m. to the sound of the life outside in the yard below. The idea of a class meeting did not fill me with a sense of joy and elation, I hadn't been near a large group of young children since I was one, and I was about to meet 30 of them, possibly all at once. When I ventured out of my room, along the corridor of the stark building, down the stairs, through the lobby and then stepped out through the double glass doors into the yard, I put my forearm up across my eyes, to shield the glare from the sun; and with that first step, the yard suddenly fell under a shroud of silence as if every child had stopped what they were doing. They had been sweeping and watering the dust ridden ground of the courtyard, or playing in the haze of the morning. Every gaze fell upon me, tumbleweed rolled past across the dusty earth in the gentle breeze, as a solitary bell began to chime slowly in the distance.

The sound of a twig breaking underfoot echoed around the court yard as a small dark haired, brown eyed boy turned towards me; he put his outstretched hand to meet mine and said the words "Buenas días Señor, me encanta conocerle",[i] the tension was broken, and the resounding bell fell silent, far away.

As I walked through the crowd of children, they greeted me one by one; they shook my hand and wished me good day, in an incredibly polite and respectful way. I wasn't expecting to be received with such warmth; the children were so genteel it was quite uplifting. I ventured into the kitchen through the dining hall and introduced myself to the two women who were busying themselves preparing breakfast, in what was a well organised kitchen and pantry; they were both rather accommodating and welcoming, I was allowed an instant coffee, something of a luxury I imagined as everything had to be accounted for in the orphanage. A couple of the children were laying the tables, so I joined them and helped set the cutlery and plates on the long narrow tables in the dining area. We put out warm cups of a sort of porridge; then we placed bread rolls and fruit at each of the many places along the long narrow tables, to be set ready for the children, all was incredibly clean and uncomplicated.

The kitchen and dining hall were fairly sparse; the kitchen was clean and functional with an adjoining storeroom, where there was a huge fridge; the dining hall was decorated in the manner of a classroom. The floors were a practical concrete painted green and the walls were adorned with a few posters, including a photo of the late middle-aged English couple who founded the orphanage, looking down upon us through their beaming sincerity. A few large glass-fronted cabinets sat along a couple of the walls, full of books and the normal paraphernalia that might be found in any school room. The surviving remnants of the former underlying inhabitants were placed on a shelf in one of the glass cabinets; it was clear that only a few ceramic artefacts remained intact.

At shortly before 7.30 a.m. the youngsters were called in; they sat very quietly at their designated places along both sides of the two tables that passed along the sides of the room with members of staff placed at either end, as was I. Mealtimes were overseen by the boss of the day. That day Lucy, a short broad woman with a genial but strict manner, sat at the top table at the end of the room that faced the double doors at the entrance. Was I in a scene from *Oliver Twist*? That remained to be seen.

As I took my seat at one end of a long table, the children hardly spoke, quietly subdued in the way they may be in a classroom. Then Lucy gestured to one of the girls of about fourteen, to say grace; after which I was introduced to Brian, who sat to my left, a well presented young man also of around fourteen, with a dark complexion and his sister Rebecca, seven, of equal complexion, who was very pretty, with short dark hair and big brown eyes, who sat to my right. Then we all began to eat, and occasionally Lucy, sat at the head table behind me, would make some profound statements about discipline and how they may be poor but they could still be respectable and dignified. It was an eye-opening experience; those children seemingly had nothing, but they were all really well behaved; charming, and courteous, they always seemed to be smiling. When I had cleaned my plate, I stood up, walked to the head table, and in the ensuing silence, of course, I said, "Please Miss, Can I have some more?"

After a breakfast of a cup full of Peruvian porridge, bread rolls with jam and fresh fruit, all the kids but two or three got up and left. I helped those two or three with their duty rota to clear the plates and do the washing up; they didn't complain they just did their work with beaming faces, and they made me laugh.

At around 8.30 a.m. the younger half of the children left for school in their tidy, smart, medium-blue and deep yellow uniforms, all the girls with their hair tied up in bows or buns held together with matching yellow braid, they were all very well presented. The second more senior shift, which went to school in the afternoon, began doing their homework in the dining hall, or going to some classes in the compound, when all the chores were said and done.

The problem I had was that I was suffering from jetlag so when all the plates were washed and tidied away, and the dining room was cleaned, I went back to bed until about 11.00 a.m..

* * *

When I resurfaced I was fortunate enough to be introduced to Mindi, a slim, serene, genteel Peruvian girl of around twenty two, who had a dark complexion and huge brown eyes; she was employed as an English teacher and was just finishing off a class. I needed to get a few things and she volunteered to take me downtown on the bus, to buy but a few essentials, such as underpants and shaving gear.

We said our farewells and walked out onto the sandy streets of the shanty town to set out upon a great adventure. We were to take the 20 minute bus trip along the busy dance of the hazy, three lane freeway, to the hustle and bustle of the markets of a major shopping centre, a few miles towards the centre of town.

We alighted at a lively shopping quarter, where Mindi led me along a vibrant street into a huge covered market where every type of food could be found. There were fresh vegetables, fruit, fish and many varieties of meat on sale, except, I noticed, there were not too many sausages; the Peruvians don't seem to be big into sausages. There were all types of electrical goods on sale, there were products that ranged from tools to clothing available in each designated section of the market, and there were bootleg CD's of any film you could think of, for Sol. 5 apiece. No doubt some of the products may not have been entirely kosher. We were coaxed by numerous amicable street sellers along the way, but I didn't find the throng of the place threatening at all, as some might think of a third world thoroughfare. Mindi and I shared ten delicious hard boiled quail eggs sold, as usual, with a chilli salsa; often seen and readily available from the street merchants in Lima, and elsewhere in Peru, for only a few Sol.

We walked through the huge closed markets until we found Mindi's family clothing stall where I bought some underpants for very little in English terms, probably only a couple of quid each, if that. We then walked back to cross a footbridge over the six lane highway into a large modern, shiny brand new, air conditioned supermarket, where I bought my shaving kit; it was the kind of store you might find in any other part of the overdeveloped, sanitised world of the Twenty First Century, with special offers to boot.

* * *

The orphanage was very well organised, the older children would have lunch at a first sitting. Then at around the time that they are leaving, the morning shift would return from school and have lunch at a second sitting. After lunch they would spend the afternoon playing around or doing their homework.

When we got back at about 1.45 p.m., on one of the 10p buses, we had missed the second sitting; but fortunately lunch had been kept aside for us. This was primarily very kind and secondly it was an absolutely delicious type of Peruvian chicken-fried rice. Mindi was quite curious about England, and I am quite curious about Peru so we had plenty to discuss before she had to leave that afternoon. She told me that she wanted to come to England to study, but money being what it is, she was unlikely to be able to afford to go there ever, which I suppose is the difference between the poverty of the third world and the wealth of the first. Most people in Europe can afford to go abroad at some time or another, but for the average Peruvian, travel overseas is highly unlikely, it is quite simply beyond their means.

When Mindi had left I was somewhat at a loose end, so I read until mid-afternoon, when Carolina strolled in to the compound with Marianela, who was a particularly voluptuous woman in her late thirties. She was a member of the Orphanage Committee, which consisted of various representatives who voted on matters pertaining, at a meeting on every Monday afternoon. Marianela spoke almost perfect English and was incredibly generous in her manner, as well as in her curves. We sat around a table outside, in the warmth of the afternoon haze and they told me what they had planned for me.

My job whilst in Lima, was I thought, to assist a team of young people from Yorkshire in the construction of a soup kitchen in a shanty town borough, in Lima, not too far from the orphanage. It soon became apparent that I was somewhat mistaken. Carolina had other plans for me because the construction team in Lima was apparently big enough and I would be more useful elsewhere.

It came as some surprise that the following day I was to catch a 14 hour bus ride that would pass over the Andes to a place called Chalhuanca, which is situated in the Apurimac Valley on the other side of the Cordillera of the Andes en route[ii] to Cuzco. I was to be met there by Carolina's husband, Juan Carlos, who would take me up into the mountains in a taxi along a narrow dirt road, to a small village called Apuquri, which rests high in the Andes. Whilst there, I was to assist in the construction of a Casa Hogar (a dormitory shelter); to enable some of the local children from the surrounding mountain villages, to get an education. Clearly it was totally impractical for the youngsters to walk as much as five or six hours a day on a round trip to go to school.

I asked Carolina and Marianela "How high exactly is Apuquri?"[iii] They smiled and said, "A bit higher than Cuzco."

"So I won't be able to breathe," I said. I had been to Cuzco the previous year and I knew that meant that the air would be incredibly thin. "Well you won't be able to breath at first" they said, still smiling,

"But after a while you'll be fine."

"But isn't the Apurimac valley famous for harbouring Narcotraficantes?"[iv]

"Well yes, we think so, but they shouldn't be a problem, some of them are really rather pleasant." "Well that's some consolation, I feel a whole lot better in the knowledge that some of the drug traffickers shouldn't be a problem because some of them are really rather pleasant."

"And what's the food like?"

"Horrible" they said in unison. I asked if there was a computer "No"

"Is there a shop?"

"We think so" and "So is there anything to do in the evenings?"

"No" they said together, and "How is the weather there?"

"It's quite warm during the day and very cold at night" and then "Oh and by the way, the village is at least an hour from the nearest proper road, you have to drive up a cliff-side track to get there" said Carolina, cheerfully.

They also took great pleasure in telling me, with big smiles on their big faces, that the locals speak a mixture of Quechua and Spanish, so I may or may not understand them, and they weren't sure where I would sleep but they were sure I would find somewhere. They also told me that there was no medical service to speak of, no police and last, but not least by any stretch of the imagination, they didn't know if I would be able to buy a .... beer!

I turned to them and asked "You seriously want me to go into the interior of Peru on a dodgy old bus, probably full of chickens, that was going to pass right up through the mountains, along cliff edges, to spend a month in a place that is so high up that the air is so thin it will be difficult to breathe; the region is full of drug dealers, I have no idea where I am to eat or sleep, the evenings will be redundant, I will freeze at night, the food will be terrible, there is no computer and there may not be any beer?"

"Well, yes" was the reply.

If that wasn't bad enough they both assured me that I would be able to look over mountain precipices as the bus ran up to over 5000 metres above sea level, en route over the cordillera, to my destination. They saw the look of alarm on my face and realised the idea of me travelling to such a desolate place was, to them, absolutely hilarious.

I said, "You're not exactly selling this are you?"

They said, still smiling, "Well no, but don't worry, if you don't like it you can always come back after a week and do some work in the orphanage."

I said, "What do you mean if? Of course I'm not going to like it." Carolina and Marianela just laughed and laughed at the prospect of me having to go to live in such a remote, poverty-stricken community.

They were laughing so much that I turned to them and told them that they really had to stop taking the Michael, though I may actually have used slightly stronger terminology. I knew little of Peru and the thought of living in the mountains caused me some not inconsiderable apprehension. I soon realised that it was highly likely that I might not actually be able to last very long, so far from the 21st century. When they saw the look of consternation on my face, Carolina and Marianela relented somewhat. Though this was some consolation, in my mind it would be an admission of failure to give up half way through the project and come back to Lima. The thought of this excursion far away from what I thought was normality, did not exact a peaceful easy feeling, but I would have to grit my teeth and do my best to bear it.

And so it seemed that I was not exactly looking forward to a month in an all-purpose luxury tourist complex. This external cultural visit was not the most secure prospect and there was another matter which was, without wishing to put too fine a point on it, the cause of some justifiable trepidation. I knew that the Apurimac Valley was a centre of cocaine production in Peru. The local growers of coca are of no concern at all, the crops are legal because the use of coca is ingrained in the Peruvian culture, not least because coca leaves are chewed by the locals as a natural antidote to altitude sickness. However coca has other uses of a recreational nature, for which an increase in coca production was required and all that was needed was for the existing crops to be augmented, albeit substantially. Land is not in short supply in Peru and coca has been grown in the

Apurimac valley since time immemorial, and before. The only problem, slight though it may have been, was that the production of refined cocaine is illegal and regrettably that, on occasion, the Narcotraficantes are not purported to be the most amenable of people. It was all too clear that they might not take too kindly to the prying eyes of a foreign visitor.

Nonetheless, despite any reservations that I may have had, Carolina reserved a ticket for me to take a bus that left for Chalhuanca, in the Apurimac Valley, at 4.30 the following afternoon.

* * *

The afternoon shift filed in through the steel gate at around five, the children were in high spirits as usual, resplendent in their blue and yellow uniforms. I went into the kitchen and helped prepare the evening meal that mainly consisted of potatoes, covered in a very agreeable savoury cream sauce, with a healthy vegetable soup to start. We ate at around six and during the meal I again sat with seven year old Rebecca who, as before, was to sit at my right hand side for every mealtime; to my left was to sit her fourteen year old brother, Brian, who it turned out, would soon had to leave the orphanage, apparently because he was about to develop the tendencies of a young Jack Russell terrier going through puberty. They were both really funny, we generally laughed a lot. Rebecca asked me to practice the times tables with her, so we began by my asking 3 times 1, and up through to the seven and eight times tables. She would count on her fingers when the numbers got bigger and was delighted when she got the answers right and delighted when I frowned at her when she got them wrong. I think sometimes she got the numbers wrong deliberately so that I would be gruff with her, because she laughed so much when I made out that I was annoyed. Rebecca was delightful.

I wasn't laughing too much however, when I asked about the ancient Inca pots that were in the cupboard. Brian told me that the orphanage was built on an ancient Inca cemetery. When they had dug the foundations for the orphanage buildings, they had found several tombs. Brian repeated the story that at the time, when the authorities were notified, they didn't care. So the builders had made a big pile of rubble and smashed about seventy ancient Inca vases; which were sent away in a skip. That broke my heart, because, as before, I knew if those vases could have been sold, the money could have funded the orphanage for quite some time; not to mention the loss of such irreplaceable historic artefacts. I then discovered that several other items had disappeared at the hands of one of the previous prominent staff members. At first blush that appeared to be a little untoward, but the authorities were not interested at the time and if those items hadn't been taken they would probably have been destroyed and sent to the tip; this at least meant that all had not been destroyed. In fact it seemed that something could be found in some recompense. Brian reliably informed me that he knew of the whereabouts of at least three more tombs within the walled perimeters of the compound that was the orphanage.

After dinner I helped clear the plates and do the washing up. It is hard to describe just how pleasant everyone was in that place. The staff were good company and took a great deal of pleasure in ribbing me over my English ways. When all the work was said and done, I sat down and succumbed to the demands of little Fanny who insisted that I give her a reading lesson; she was an orphan of around five years old, she was tiny, very sensitive and gentle in her way. I talked to a few of the other kids who were very curious about England and Europe in general. They told me about their country and how school was, just like any child might do. Some of the children were allowed to watch a little TV whilst the others undertook various activities, such as running around like lunatics and throwing wooden spinning tops to the ground which seemed to be de rigueur;[v] they all disappeared, almost at once, to wash and go to bed at around 9.00 p.m.

As the night had fallen at around 7.00 p.m. and as the evening progressed, the dogs could be heard in the distance of the surrounding streets. After tea with Lucy and Philippa in the cool of the evening, I went to bed shortly after 9.30, when all went quiet in the compound. I could hear loud music through my window, being played just outside the walls, where there was a small street party going on. Fortunately the celebrations ended shortly before midnight, shortly before I had finished reading. Then I got myself off to sleep, which was not difficult at all, I'd had a good day and jetlag was setting in, once more.

Thursday 3rd September

I woke up at about 5.30 a.m. to the sound of the children outside in the yard below. I got dressed and walked out into the warm hazy sunshine of the early morning, as was the normal climate for that time of year in Lima, derived from the incessant pollution. I got myself a coffee from the kitchen and helped with the breakfast; which was basic but nourishing, and of course I asked if I could have some more. Following grace, Lucy, the boss, gave a lesson in morality to the quiet spoken children during breakfast. I stole some of Rebecca's breakfast when she wasn't looking, then she stole some of mine; Rebecca and I practiced some more times tables, I think we got up to number seven. Brian was his usual jovial self, the other young girls on my table were smiling a lot and asking me questions in a very giggly way, they were all very entertaining.

After breakfast I helped clear the tables, assisted with the washing up and I swept the floor. I then filled up the bins across the courtyard. When the clearing up was done I thought I'd better clean myself. So I took a shower after the first shift had left for school. I couldn't really use the bathroom at the same time as the children. I thought it prudent to wait until they were gone.

When I was eventually clean, I was shown around the newest whitewashed building by one of the staff, Sarah, a young English teacher of around twenty three, who was very helpful. She showed me the bedrooms on the upper floors of the first new building that were to be used mainly by

39

volunteers from England. It was the unpaid helpers that provided most of the income for the charity. If they made sufficient contribution[vi] a volunteer would be allowed the opportunity to work for the project and pay Sol. 7 a night for the privilege, not a bad thing at all.

The ground floor of the main building had the infrastructure of a kitchen, which was about to be filled with second hand computers donated from England. Adjacent was an open area about the size of a large classroom that could be used for various things such as rehearsals for the Christmas play. It wasn't quite finished, it was whitewashed, the floors were tiled and it clearly had potential. Attached to one end of the building were a couple of smaller rooms that could be used as small classrooms, and beside those was a large garage-like area that was used to store goods that had been sent over by the charity from England.

That morning I tidied up and packed my bags in preparation for my journey into the mountains, not that I had much more than a rucksack. I was to leave non essentials locked up in Carolina's office for safe keeping. I then sat around a while, talked to some of the children and read some Spanish; then I gave little Fanny a reading lesson for about half an hour before lunch.

Lunch consisted of a delectable plate of tuna with vegetables and mash; Becky and Brian were just as good company as always. Becky and I went through sometimes tables as had become our habit; she was getting quite good. As always she would sometimes deliberately get an answer wrong because she knew I would grimace at her in retribution, which made her laugh, a lot. When the meal was over I helped clear up, swept the floors and gave tiny, cute, little Fanny another reading lesson; then I checked my packing again and I read for a while. I talked to the kids and staff about nothing in particular whilst I waited to be taken across town to the bus station later that afternoon.

Carolina and Marianela rolled up at around 2.30 p.m. in a great mood. I guess it was quite amusing to send the Gringo over the soaring Andes into the middle of nowhere. I collected my bags and the three of us took a taxi for about an hour along the madness of the freeway through to the other side of the centre of town to one of several bus stations. It was incredible to be driving across such a vibrant third world city. The taxi danced through the traffic, to the sound of various horns, until the traffic slowed as we arrived at the more narrow congested streets in the centre. When we arrived at the bus station, they told me to be careful of my bags because the pickpockets and thieves were rife in the district. Marianela and Carolina were fabulous; they were always upbeat as they directed me to buy some drinks, sweets and biscuits for the journey. I got on the bus and had only just taken my place by the window, when my fellow Peruvian traveller asked me if I would exchange seats. Carolina and Marianela told me not to move, I'm not sure why; we talked through the window while we waited for the bus to finally leave, then they waved me out of the station. As the bus left the station I felt a calm apprehension of what was to become of my trip, as I sat on the somewhat rustic sleeper bus, with its overhead TV screens along the central aisle, vociferous in Peruvian Spanish. My travel companion who sat beside me was a man from the countryside, a campesino, who had been spending some time on holiday in Lima with relatives. He was polite and very civil; he said little and knew nothing of the world outside Peru that I live in.

After a trip of around half an hour along the dusty city streets, the bus left the confines of the town, down south along the long distant, empty rolling desert highways via Nazca then high up into the cold, harsh, sparsely populated Andes; the bus drove slowly up along the narrow metalled roads that wound their way along the sides of numerous cliff edges that looked down upon the clouds. Needless to say the journey did not have the safest of reputations. I drifted in and out of sleep, and sometimes I would choke myself awake, gasping for oxygen, because the air was so thin.

I awoke at about 4.00 a.m. as the sun arose and we drove into the grey stone maze of Puquio; a rustic, low rise, high altitude city, adorned with the kind of large vibrant graffiti that would sit very well in a revolutionary seventies movie. As the sun cast its early morning shadows on the unkempt streets of Puquio we drove up into the mountains above, where we stopped a while looking down on the isolated city. It was a wonder to behold; gazing upon the steep slopes of the valley below where sits the sun soaked conurbation. It seemed to the average bystander that it could well have been "Scorchio" in Puquio quite often. At college I used to drink in a pub called the "Chequers at Well", a tiny Hampshire village. "Puquio" means "Well" in Quechua, the name may have had identical meaning, but the culture was different of course. I imagine the beer and the Porky Scratchings were not quite the same.

Though we had been given a few coca sweets to help with the lack of oxygen at altitude, they didn't seem to help me very much. When we had stopped in the heights above, as we looked down upon the city, we got out to stretch our legs or have a surreptitious piss in the scrubland. Even a short walk around the bus left me to gasp, quite short of breath. Fortunately we weren't at such altitude quite long enough to cause me a real problem. It was quite apparent that it was not a place that I would recommend to go jogging; in fact it wasn't a good idea to move around too quickly at all.

Though it is difficult to ascertain who is susceptible to it, until it is upon you, acute mountain sickness or Hypobaropathy, is caused by low partial oxygen pressure at high altitude, which normally only occurs at over 2,400 metres above sea level. This can develop into High Altitude Pilmonery Edema of High Altitude Cerebral Edema, both of which are potentially fatal. Chronic mountain sickness or Monge's disease is a different condition that may develop after prolonged exposure to high altitude. The symptoms are similar to "flu, carbon monoxide poisoning or a hangover", but still and potentially deadly.

Apparently the main problem with altitude is not the descent; it is a rapid ascent that can create difficulties. If there is a gradual exposure to increased altitude the blood begins to produce higher levels of haemoglobin, which are the red corpuscles that soak up oxygen like a sponge. This change will enable the body to acclimatise to the low oxygen levels at altitude. This may be why people, who live in the mountains, do appear to be so incredibly fit, and may often live to a ripe old age; often to over 100 years.

When we set off once more a young slim uniformed waitress served a sparse sweet bread roll and a very thin filter coffee for breakfast, after which I managed to grab a little sleep. It wasn't long before we arrived in the remote town of Chalhuanca that sat in the sharp, dazzling sunshine of the spectacular Apurimac[vii] Valley, carved by the river Apurimac, which was apparently brimming with trout. At around 6.00 a.m., I stepped down from the bus into the main square that rested beneath the imposing cordillera that rose high above us.

Chalhuanca, is the capital of the seventeen Distritos of the Aymares Province in the Apurimac region, which is blessed with a vast population of less than 1000. It seemed to be a magical peaceful place, far from the stresses and strains of the sterile day to day, computerised existence of the modern world. Some say that the name Chalhuanca comes from the fish called Chai Hua in Quechua, abundant in that part of the world, but it most likely comes from the name of the same fish, the name having changed to "Chal" over time, and "Huanca", named after the stones in a nearby Huayco.[viii]

Friday 4ᵗʰ September

There was a young man of about thirty waiting, stocky at about five foot seven with long dark curly hair and a friendly broad smiling face. He looked at me from beneath his straw cowboy hat and simply said, "Philips?" I was glad to see him, even if he did add an "s" to my name. After such a long journey I didn't want to have to wait around wondering when I was going to be met in such a distant town. Juan Carlos was a very amenable bloke, he took me to have some breakfast in the centre of town, which was a most welcome thing. We stepped down from the busy street into what seemed to be a small front room, with a few sparse wooden tables and chairs in it, with its own agreeable waitress, who directed us to sit down adjacent to the front window that looked out at the passers-by. We shared the café with four other customers, probably the only other clientele that could fit into the place, it was in effect packed to the gunnels.

There wasn't a great deal of choice on the menu. The clientele could generally decide between plain chicken broth, chicken broth a la carte, or chicken broth of the day, all of which did appear to be the same dish. So we decided to have chicken broth, which was a very good chicken broth in fact. The "Full Peruvian" is in fact the common choice for breakfast in Peru, for obvious reasons. It had a clean, fresh tasting organic flavour about it and was incredibly nourishing. The Peruvians tend not to fillet the chicken, it is not an art that they are accustomed to; they just chop it up and put it in the pot, nothing is thrown away apart from the

45

head and feathers. In fact half an egg can sometimes be seen in the soup, cooked where it grew, inside the carcass.

When we had eaten our delicious chicken broth breakfast, I felt a whole lot better. The air was thin, my body needed to acclimatise and Juan Carlos needed to collect his luggage. So we walked a short distance across the street, to his old rustic hotel where we walked through the narrow corridors and cleared his charming, wooden floored room, of his few worldly goods. While Juan Carlos attended to something that I am not quite sure of, I spent half an hour in sufferance of the addiction of an internet café nearby. Amidst the tedium of attempting to get some sense out the University and other bureaucratic nonsense, I wrote to my girlfriend to tell her I was OK, but in truth she had never been happy about me going to South America. She didn't seem too willing to write, which was probably because she hadn't wanted me to leave, which was quite understandable, but not entirely reasonable from my perception of things, because I was only to be away a few months. No doubt a member of the female gender could explain it to me; however I am sure I would never fully understand.

When all was ready we met as arranged in the street by the hotel entrance and very quickly found a taxi. It was an old dark blue Japanese estate car that we were fortunate enough to share with an attractive young female doctor who seemed to appear from nowhere and happened to be on her way to Apuquri, quite by coincidence. I soon learned that she was to assist in the medical centre in the village for a couple of weeks. She told me that Peru has a "National Health Service" where everything is free, up to a point. That is, I suppose, if you can find anyone to administer the required health care.

46

The taxi drove along the highway out of town alongside the river Apurimac that had gouged a deep spectacular ravine over thousands of years. We were of course entertained by the obligatory radio station playing crackling Peruvian music in the background; we drove for about ten or fifteen minutes south, along the river, then we turned back up a rough, dusty grey single track gravel road that had been carved into the side of a mountain. I was impressed by the intensity of the day, the sun was getting warmer, and we began to feel the heat; the driver seemed entirely unconcerned about anything at all. The fact that we might be driving along a cliff edge, inches from certain death, seemed inconsequential, of that I was in no doubt. The driver seemed entirely oblivious to this peril, I imagine his middle name was Fangio. Nonetheless, I was secure in the knowledge that we had an effigy of the Virgin Mary on the dashboard and a cross hanging from the rear view mirror.

As we drove along the dirt road, from time to time we passed by a couple of men or women along the way, moving a few donkeys or cows up the road. They were very happy to see us, the people in the mountains are a spiritual people, it was not a chore for them to walk with livestock in the mountains it seemed to be a pleasure. I noticed the occasional small adobe dwelling en route set back from the roadside, but not much else aside from the scrub, a few boulders and the occasional fresh water stream that flowed beside or across the track.

Following around 45 minutes of a fairly hot, sweaty and hairy drive up the dusty cliff side with our friend Fangio, we turned a corner and were confronted with the metropolis that is Apuquri, looming above us; population 406. We drove up past the lawn fronted medical centre that was set back at the bottom of town. We continued up into the centre that consisted of a small plaza, in the standard star like form that is commonplace in the region, with a concrete football pitch on the far side. There was a row of houses containing a two story municipal building along the left hand side of the road that ran alongside the plaza and the pitch. On the opposite side was a large corrugated iron roofed church situated in front of the school set behind. The concrete pitch was bordered at the top and left side, by two tiers of large concrete steps that were used for seating at football matches and council meetings. The lower ran alongside the ornamental square with its central bandstand and pathways in the shape of a diagonal cross. The adobe dwellings of the village rose up from behind the pitch and the concrete tiers adjacent to the church. It was as though they were a part of an American film score, depicting the plight of the war torn, oppressed by a Military Junta.

The streets of the village were merely rock strewn dirt tracks wide enough for a small lorry; there were also several steep foot paths that climbed up between the few rows of unkempt adobe houses that ascended from the centre. There were several people going about their business in the streets, a few dogs and the occasional group of cows or sheep being taken along a pathway. Apuquri was a peaceful, tranquil mountain village that looked down upon the Apurimac valley in the distance beneath us.

To the east of the village lies the mountain named Apu San Francisco[ix] a fertile place from where the sun rises, and fresh water springs. The local people believe that the ancient Inca live in a lost city within it; by this they may mean in spirit and not in the physical sense that one may imagine. To the west in the distance looms Apu Ronco,[x] a black mountain, a dark foreboding place, where the sun sets and nothing ever grows. At the foot of the peak lies a lake, where the water appears to be black, due to the darkness beneath. It is said that if you are to drink the water, the mountain will consume you. Livestock is known to have often disappeared over the years and when I asked if anyone had climbed it, I was told, "Oh yes, many people have climbed it .... but they have never been seen again."

* * *

We dropped the esteemed doctor off by the plaza; I didn't ever see her again. Perhaps she drank the water. We continued through the centre of town up a dusty rock filled street that swept up to the left past that houses around the top of the town. We alighted near a local municipal building which was one of the few that had been built out of concrete and actually had a solid floor. The vast majority of the buildings in the village were made of adobe, where dry earth lay underfoot, nothing more.

The view was spectacular from the dizzy heights of the tiny village. We had risen to such an elevated place that the large powerful Apurimac River appeared along the brown and grey valley bottom that led into a thin grey thread of cotton in the distance beneath us. Chalhuanca and the rest of the World had long since disappeared from sight, as had any normal oxygen density within the air.

Juan Carlos and I walked, when I say walked, I mean I staggered, I could hardly breathe, into the sparse main room of the building where there was a large wooden table at one end and very little else. It was in effect the village hall. "There you go" said Juan Carlos with a big smile on his face,

"That is your bed for the month" in Spanish of course. I told him he had to be joking, in Spanish of course. I didn't want to sleep on a table in the Village hall, I needed some sort of bedding and maybe we could find a mattress somewhere. Juan Carlos showed me his room adjacent, where he had a spare mattress on the top bunk of his bed. After some persuasion he relented, after all he couldn't sleep on two mattresses on two bunks at once; it stands to reason. So it probably wasn't going to be so bad after all. I had the comfort of my sleeping bag, and a possible mattress to sleep on, in the village hall, on a table. That said I had no idea what we were going to do for food, I saw only the partial remnants of a camping gas stove with a double ring for a kitchen.

We left the bags in the council building and walked down the slope at the front where I was shown the outside toilet, in fact they were all outside. This one was relatively posh, it was made of porcelain but of course there was no seat or lock, it didn't flush, but it did have a door. This was the lap of luxury.

There were three men working on a steep grassy slope that fell below us, they looked pretty wild to the Western eye, which is ironic, we were, in fact, in the West. They had dark hair, dark skin and dark eyes and were covered in a mid-tan mud. They were mixing a great pile of standard mid-tan mud with a fine straw by walking around in it in their bare feet, with their trousers rolled up around their knees. The kind of cleansing reflexological mud bath that will lift the spirits, normally only affordable to the ladies that lunch in the West End of London (there are other cities available). These men were all full of life, smiling and telling jokes amongst themselves as they walked around in the mire.[xi] They were taking handfuls of mud and pressing it into a wooden mould

50

that was an oblong frame of about 9 by 9 by 24 inches; about the same size and shape as an English hod that would carry twelve bricks. When packed full they would then lift the wooden frame leaving a wet adobe brick that would be left out in the sun for a week or so before it would dry enough to be used in construction. There were many neat rows of adobe bricks laid out across the slope beside them, increasing in number as they worked. When we approached the men, they introduced themselves cordially to me and made several incredibly courteous gestures, which for the most part I did not understand, not least because the vernacular was a mixture of Spanish and the local Quechua dialect, the language most common to the Inca. But I did notice that they were incredibly polite; they were perfect gentlemen, and they were all covered in mid-tan mud.

After an exchange of politeness, a lot of smiles and a few invitations, Juan Carlos and I bid our farewells and walked (I still staggered for lack of oxygen) back up the hill into the council building to have a lunch which consisted of some good quality bread and cheese that I had bought off a street vendor in Chalhuanca, for very little money. Following our cordon bleu repast we walked down past the modest low slung bullring[xii] that sat upon the hill just above of our dwelling, which was in fact the town hall.

We walked up very slowly, the air was very thin, still higher along the steep dusty streets to a house that stood above the road opposite a tiny shop about ten minutes' walk from the centre, though in my case probably an hour's walk. There was a small lawn adjacent to the pretty little adobe house and the owner came out to greet us as we ascended the five or so stone steps. Marie Paz, (a first name meaning Maria of Peace) was a petite slim dark haired woman of middle age, she had an incredibly gentle most serene manner about her and promptly told Juan Carlos that I was to have a room in her house whilst I was staying in Apuquri. That was a genuine surprise, I thought it must have been my birthday, in actual fact, I was right, it was my birthday. That was a proper result; I hadn't really been looking forward to sleeping on a table for a month, albeit with the luxury of a mattress, sharing the sparse quarters that Juan Carlos had so kindly provided for me.

So of course, Juan Carlos and I went back down to the municipal hall and collected all of my few belongings. I have a sneaking suspicion Juan Carlos wasn't too happy about that, he must have been a little jealous in retrospect. We got back to Marie Paz's house after about twenty minutes. I think I may have illustrated the point that it was not so easy for me to move too quickly; the air was so sparse I was often out of breath and had to rest on the way. When we got back to Marie Paz's place I settled into my room, where my bed was made with seven blankets. I was to share it with a couple of guinea pigs that had a free run of the house and a year's worth of dried wooden scrub piled up along a wall, that was to be used as firewood. The custom in rural Peru is to keep guinea pigs that eat all the peelings and generally anything else edible that may be dropped on the kitchen floor or elsewhere for that matter; then when fat enough, the guinea pigs themselves are despatched and skinned over a hot cauldron, then they are roasted as a delicacy for a special occasion, such as the Queen's birthday. A perfect form of recycling without the use of bins, you quite simply eat the recycling system.

When all was settled, Marie Paz and I walked down the incline through town to the building site on the edge of town beneath us, which is where we were to continue the construction of the dormitory shelter, the reason for my visit.

A team from the RAF had dug out and filled the concrete foundations for the construction of the building a few weeks beforehand and were long gone. When Marie Paz and I arrived there was a group of half a dozen men who had begun to build the thick rusty mud brown adobe walls of what was to be quite a large building of two large adjoining dormitories, male and female, a couple of bathrooms, male and female, a kitchen, an office and a large dining area adjacent.

The men were all really scruffy, such as is befitting for poor construction workers who were not about to be wearing their Sunday best at work. It was clearly fashionable to wear a fedora, a trilby or a baseball cap and their clothes with a layer of grime all over them, which is understandable considering the profession involved. They were not the tallest of people, some might say that they were vertically challenged, being mostly between 5ft and 5ft 6 ins. tall.

What was impressive was that they were all incredibly strong and incredibly healthy. Later, when I began to work alongside them, it soon became apparent that they could carry huge weight upon their shoulders without any difficulty at all.

I was introduced to Don Fernando and Roger, who were both powerful, short stocky men, around 5ft 2 ins tall, in their mid-thirties. They had European features but with dark complexions. They had dark brown skin, dark brown eyes and short dark brown hair. Peso was a quiet teenager with the same dark features as had Sebas who was in his mid-twenties; he had the manner of someone who was always joking. Juan Visconti (AKA Hercules) had a slim wiry

53

physique and a couple of his bedraggled front teeth were missing. Juan Visconti had the complexion of an Italian, I think there must have been a clue in the name, and it wasn't Hercules. Constantino was the older man amongst us, an octogenarian, he had a walking stick, he appeared to be of Caucasian origin, and was around 5ft 6" tall with curly greying hair.

I was about to learn that almost everyone that I was about to meet in this town was "simpático", or someone who is willing to please, like Sister Theresa for example. This is as opposed to people who are "antipático", the antonym which would refer to people like Hitler or Mussolini, for example, or your average 1970's or 80's mother-in-law according to the comedic humour of the time. Strangely though, it seems that since the onset of political correctness all mothers-in-law have become incredibly nice people. I would never suggest otherwise, but as they say, many a true word spoken in jest.

The guys I was about to work with were marvellous; when they were told that it was my birthday they all sang "Happy Birthday Dear Gringo" in Spanish, in unison, which was highly amusing. This meant that we also had to go for a drink to celebrate; so we cleared up the tools and the work of the day and walked together up into town, which meant up one block and take a left. We arrived at a rustic corner shop that was too small for us all to sit in, so the proprietor opened up a room adjacent, at the next door down the street. Along the sidewall of the large grey, earthen floored room was a long wooden table with benches on both sides. It was a large old dust filled place with a few cooking implements lying around at one end, an old portable stereo on some

54

otherwise empty wooden shelves, the odd wooden table, two cases of beer, one glass and a bottle opener.

Being the relatively wealthy European I took it upon myself to buy them a case of twelve 16oz bottles of beer, whereupon we were provided with another small glass. The custom in rural Peru is to fill the glass with beer, pour a little on the floor in salute to Pachamama,[xiii] pass the bottle to the guy on your left, almost empty the glass, pour the last drop on the floor, again in salute to Pachamama,[xiv] then pass it on; that is until the bottle is empty, which it often was. I thought this may have originated in a similar way to the old naval custom, of the passing of port to the left. It was customary to open another, and then another, until everything was drunk and everyone was drunk. It became apparent that when a drink was taken in Apuquri, we practiced the same custom with beers and spirits, or any other drink that was available for that matter. It seemed that being plastered[xv] in Apuquri was far more common than I had expected. I was pleased to learn that there was no concern over the availability of the occasional beer, quite the contrary in fact.

Marie Paz had left us men, fairly rapidly in fact, to discuss male topics such as the problems of the harvests, as we sat and listened to the crackling traditional Peruvian music played by Apuquri's very own radio station. We talked about the viability of reseeding the ancient Inca terraces that covered a large chunk of the hill sides surrounding the village, which raised the question as to why virtually all of the Inca terraces that can be seen all over Peru appear to be devoid of any crop. It was quite surprising and sad to learn that the rural communities in Peru in the main, have lost the Inca secrets as to how to fully irrigate these ancient farm lands as they used to more than 500 years ago.

That is the predominant reason why many of the Inca terraces are left redundant and the community have only harvested the sloped fields which they referred to as "cákras" which were only less than half of the available cultivable farmland created by the terraces. It was disappointing to learn that even if they did discover and re-establish the irrigation channels, the campesinos[xvi] simply did not have enough money to buy all the seed that they needed; they made do with what they had. There is a certain irony that under Inca rule the people of Peru very rarely went short of food. Yet in the 21st century, it is regrettable, that when the harvests are not so good, the dogs number fewer in the streets. I am certain that the mountain people do not eat canine meat, it seems that they just could not afford to feed their pets.

I thought I might like to buy the villagers some seed, in the vain hope that they would be able to harvest far more than they did. That may seem simple enough, but they are a proud people, in Apuquri they do not wish to accept handouts from anyone.

As the evening progressed I was told that there wasn't a chemical anywhere within that community.[xvii] everything was grown in a totally natural way, and the harvest was consequently very healthy, and so were the people.

These rural people, bereft of money, lived on a diet of organic food that was entirely free from insecticides or contaminants of any kind; they produced the type of food you might find at a farmers' market in England, but with fewer pollutants. They told me that it was normal for the members of the community to live until between 95 and 105 years of age. I told them that I would return when I was eighty five to get the 20 year extension.

Constantino bought a second case of beer when the first was gone. When I had seen him at work he had used a walking stick, when not mixing adobe mud in his bare feet. They told me that he was 85 years old; still smiling and still mucking in, literally. Constantino had little choice but to work, there was no such thing as a pension available in Apuquri, it was not a concept that was understood.

A little later on, much to my delight, whilst we were drinking the second case of beer, an announcement came over the radio that there was a new man in town who had come all the way from England to support the construction project for the Casa Hogar.[xviii] This was a great celebration; I had a birthday dedication broadcast especially for me, high in the Andean airways. That memory still brings a smile to my face when I think of it; but sadly I don't remember the name of the song.

At about ten o'clock we had finished the second case of beer, and it was time to leave; so when we had bade the men farewell Juan Visconti and I walked very slowly up the steep pathway through the village to Marie Paz's house. It had been a hard slog back up the mountain slope to Marie Paz's house; the air was so meagre it was going to take quite some time to get accustomed to the altitude. When we returned to the house, Marie Paz had very kindly prepared us some fried chicken that I had bought in town that morning, cooked with herbs and served with rice. We ate our delicious late night feast, sitting outside beneath a magical, star filled deep blue sky. The stars that shine at night in the Peruvian mountains are more clear and bright than can be found anywhere else in the world, it is hard to describe quite how impressive they are. I cracked open the whisky, Celebrity chefs, eat your heart out.

Marie Paz had given me a white bucket, so I had a pot to piss in; that was designed to save me going outside into what was to become the freezing cold of the night. I would therefore hopefully avoid any opportunity of frostbite or chill in any of my extremities. The garden latrine happened to be a hole in the ground, which was on the other side of the garden, behind a wall. It had a tin roof and a view over the adjoining gardens that sloped away beneath. This was on occasion quite perturbing because the next day I discovered that it meant that you could wave to the neighbours while on the WC and they would wave to you whilst in flagrante, as it were.

Quite content and nourished I must have got to bed at around midnight. It was bitterly cold that night. I awoke several times quite simply due to the fact that I was freezing, or on occasion I was gasping for air, choking due to lack of oxygen. Much to my dismay, my hands, being the only skin apart from the face that was not covered, had become incredibly painful. I was being attacked by the virtually invisible, agonising sand flies that have a tiny bite that itches like something from the depths of hell. Sand flies should be avoided at all times; apparently they can also carry viruses that rot the flesh beneath the skin. Unfortunately for me no one had mentioned that I should bring some insect repellent. It's not the sort of thing that you expect you might need at over 3,700 metres above sea level.

Saturday 5th September

I woke up feeling tired, and slightly hungover. Perhaps the booze had hit me harder than usual due to the altitude, not least because I had not in reality drunk very much. The bites on my hands had calmed down a little but were still very painful. I guess it must have been around about 9.00 a.m. when I walked out to a breakfast that Marie Paz had prepared of porridge, tortilla and fresh bread, which was all very tasty and most welcome. The coffee was instant with a splash of condensed milk, which sweetened it ever so slightly. It was a wonderful thing, not least because there was no cow's milk and no fridge. Marie Paz had also set out a large bowl of water in the sunshine on the lawn, which she had heated for me, to have what used to be referred to as an Englishman's wash, where you basically shave and clean yourself as best you can with a flannel, some soap and a bucket of water. The sun was shining brightly down on the valley that morning, but there was a chill in the air, which made that wash just a little too refreshing.

After breakfast I was introduced to Cleo Fé, who was our next door neighbour. She was a sweet, petite old lady of around eighty four years of age, who swore a lot, in fact, most of the time. Cleo Fé was quite small; around 5 foot tall; she had the appearance of a farmer's wife dressed in black wearing the traditional fedora and many skirts, her lined face was full of character. I later learned that Cleo Fé could not read, write or indeed, count properly.

Marie Paz told me later that Cleo Fé had lost her husband some 40 years previously, and custom dictated that it wasn't the done thing to remarry. So Cleo Fé had settled herself to wearing black and caring for her pets.

We shared our lawn with her three small cows, (their ears pierced with pink tassels), her numerous chickens, her cats and their kittens, that ran about the place. We often saw one of the cows walk into her kitchen when they were hungry. Then, moments later, we would hear Cleo Fé shouting a volume of expletives at them, that is before she would chase them out through the kitchen door in reverse, arse first and around the garden, with a stick; which she generally did, much to our delight, while Marie Paz and I partook of our breakfast.

Animals were very much part of life in Apuquri, it was far away from the clinical existence of the Western world. We often had chickens in our living room, usually on the table looking for food and often eating it, which would bring us to do the same as Cleo Fé, except without quite such a big stick. Animals lived all around us. That morning, I heard Cabo, one of our adopted dogs, growling. Coaser, our resident gay dog, was trying to mount him, which Cabo didn't seem too pleased about, because he no doubt, was not a molly.[xix] I had to separate them to avoid a more violent confrontation, which was not a difficult task. On other occasions I was shown the wounds, normally in between the shoulder blades of the cattle, made by the vampire bats that came out at night. Apparently the cows didn't feel a thing, but there were stories that if a vampire bat bit a chicken, or a small animal it might bleed it dry. There are also stories of the bats biting humans, but how true these stories are I am not so sure.

It was a Saturday, I'd only just arrived and clearly I wasn't expected to work first thing. It was 3.30 p.m. by the time I'd finished sorting things out, reading and doing very little. Marie Paz, me and the dogs meandered down the mountainside path around the mid-afternoon to go to check out the building works.

As we walked down the steep rocky trail through the middle of town, everyone we passed on the way, including the smallest of children, wished us good day, in the most polite, respectful, manner. These pleasantries lightened my day somewhat, to say the least. I was introduced as the Englishman who was there to support the building project; they were all pleased to see me, as I was to them. Many things in Apuquri lift your spirits, even something as simple as walking through the village, and drinking the local hooch of course.

We went to the shop near the plaza where, under instruction from Marie Paz, I bought a big two litre bottle of Inca Cola, for Sol. 4.5 (90p), which I gave to the men when we got to the site. They earned only Sol. 25 (£5.00) a day, so to them it was a respectable gesture. We sat on a few adobe bricks and passed the bottle around, drinking from one cup, from which Pachamama was saluted in the usual way, until the bottle was empty, a most pleasant endeavour, it must be said.

The men were all fit and healthy, they all wore caps or fedora hats. They were fairly grubby in their western attire, but that was normal for any construction worker, there was little choice. They were in high spirits, all the time telling jokes in a mixture of Spanish and Quechua. Sometimes they would speak to me in pure Quechua and I would look at them and say "What the expletive are you talking about? You

61

know I can't understand any jodita Quechua" and they would smile, apologise and repeat themselves in Spanish.

Having a break in the mountains of Peru wasn't too different to sitting at break on any building site that I had experienced in England. There was a slight difference in the language of course, though the content was basically the same. In Peru they even throw away some of their drink as every professional builder does in England, where it is important to throw the last of a cup of tea on the ground, as though it were a ritual.

Marie Paz's adopted position within the project was that of a manager. I soon discovered that she would go to the site every morning and late afternoon to inspect the works and discuss the job with the men. She made sure that the job was going as close to plan as was practical.

Don Fernando and Roger seemed to be the foremen. They were the bricklayers who appeared to organise the others, and were the main consultants. Constantino mixed the mud as cement for the adobe bricks; Hercules carried the muck[xx] to the bricklayers Roger and Don Fernando. Peso and Sebas loaded out the adobe bricks, putting them in place, feeding the bricklayers, very much like any hod carrier would do on a European building site.

The job was coming along well but slowly. Adobe bricks are cemented together using the same type of mud that they are made out of mixed with a fine straw, referred to as "paja". The bricks are not entirely uniform so they have to have the top surface chipped off flat, when the mortar is dry and solidified in situ beneath the sun. This levelling of the top of the bricks has to be done with a mattock, prior to the next course being laid on top. They are quite resilient those bricks, so building walls out of adobe can take quite some time.

After we had spoken to the team Marie Paz and I walked up the hill from the site to a celebration of Pachamama at one of the local houses. This was one of many rituals practised to encourage a good harvest. The particular festivity in question was undertaken well in advance of the sowing of the cákras on the slopes high above the village. There were four pairs of long-horned bulls[xxi] in the front garden, tied in pairs by wooden yokes over their necks. These icons of the ploughing ritual were periodically blessed with small drops of spirits and other drinks poured on the ground in front of them, no doubt as a salute to Pachamama; all whilst the assembled crowd ate lots of food and consumed copious amounts of refreshing alcoholic libation.

Conversation wasn't exactly rife but I was well attended to. The older ladies would walk around offering glasses of light pink, blue or grey Chicha,[xxii] from large plastic, rather professional looking jerry cans.

When presented with a full glass of around three quarters of a pint, I had to pour a little on the ground, salute Pachamama, then I had to neck the lot, leaving just a drop to pour on the ground, again in honour of Pachamama. It wasn't too strong in taste, but this was a serious drink. The maize alcohol had an effect of making everything quite vivid, it lifted my spirits somewhat; apparently it had other properties as well. I was given a plate of rice and potatoes with a little meat, which was very basic but nutritious. They also offered shots of the local cañazo,[xxiii] and a brown liquor that they referred to as wine; both were very strong. It was important that each time I drank chicha, or indeed a shot, I drank it straight down, to avoid any possibility of offence. By the time I left I was well on the way to being well and truly plastered.

As night began to fall at around 6.15 p.m. Marie Paz and I bid our farewells. As we walked away Marie Paz and I decided that the ceremony was fundamentally a good excuse to get pissed,[xxiv] and believe me everybody there was in an excellent mood. While we walked up the hill past where the three men had been making the adobe bricks the day before, Marie Paz told me it was important to accept offers of drink, and especially food as these offers were an expression of love, and a refusal was more than likely to offend.

We were looking to find Juan Carlos in the municipal building, but there was no one at the hall and no sign of Juan Carlos, he was nowhere to be seen, which was slightly disappointing, but not unusual. This was not really the cause of much concern.

We continued up past the old bullring above and walked up along the high road until we got back home. It must have been tea time, because Marie Paz prepared some tea from the herb thyme, which is apparently good for everything, and a common brew in the mountains.

It wasn't long before Juan Carlos turned up with one of the neighbours, Olivia, a woman who wore many layers of big skirts and the standard fedora type hat. We didn't ask where he had been, clearly that would have been improper. Juan Carlos was his usual jovial self in fact, and acted as though nothing had happened, which is true because nothing had. It would have been better if he had made his presence felt in monitoring the works, but that was no great affliction.

I opened a bottle of cañazo,[xxv] part of which Juan Carlos and I mainly shared. Olivia and Marie Paz did not partake in such things very often. We talked for a while about the project and the orphanage, but Olivia didn't say very much at all and she didn't stay very long. I would not say that she was in any way whatsoever dense, but it turned out that when we talked about oxygen levels Olivia had no idea that the air was at altitude less dense and down below in Chalhuanca more dense. I wonder if she even understood that the density of air could vary at all or even what density was.

When Juan Carlos had left to sleep at the municipal hall Marie Paz and I watched a TV program about the German woman, Maria Reiche, who had spent the latter part of her life studying the Nazca lines that are found in the Nazca desert in the South Western Peru, which is not so far from Apuquri. She spent her time in this pursuit, in an attempt to unravel the mystery of how they came into being, but to no avail. The etchings were noticed by Ms. Reiche when, at the age of 35, she flew over them in the 1930's. They are so large that they can only be seen from the air and until that time were unknown to the outside world. There are approximately 650 enormous drawings and 800 lines, etched across the grey arid desert at Nazca, many are approximately 60 metres across, for example there is a monkey 90 metres across and a spider 45 metres long; the largest figures are 300 metres across; the trapezoids are perfectly straight and are several kilometres in length.

The images of various animals, birds and insects in all probability, relate to star constellations. The trapezoids, are of such size, and are so perfectly aligned, that they could easily be mistaken for the patterns of aircraft runways. These images exist to this day because the desert may have no more than half an inch of rain a year. These gargantuan etchings, carved in the desert floor, could be as much as 3500 years old, if not more, and no-one knows how they were made.

Some historians however, say that they were made by the Nazca people who, it is said, inhabited the area between 300 BC and 700 AD. This theory is portrayed because identical images appear on the ceramic work of the Nazca people, and pieces of that pottery have been found close to the lines themselves. This doesn't actually mean that the Nazca people made the images in the desert, but it does mean that they could actually see them, and how they could see them nobody knows.

Another conjecture suggests that the Nazca lines were made by extra-terrestrials; this has been corroborated by drawings of flying machines that have been discovered of Indian and Egyptian origin dating back as far as five thousand years. Objects that appear to represent flying machines have also been found in South America, where the oldest known man-made structures are seven thousand years old. Nonetheless it remains a mystery as to how the Nazca lines came to be.

Something else interesting about Nazca is that in and around the desert, where rain barely falls, there is an incredibly sophisticated, ancient underground irrigation system that is likely to be a well over 2,500 years old. The network of wells is strategically placed to draw water that is taken from the nearby mountains, to irrigate pastures. The locality was at one time abundant in normal crops such as potatoes and maize, and also crops such as the grapevine, which were used to make wine. Today these systems are sadly redundant, but fortunately are in the process of renovation, possibly due to the rise in tourism in the area during the past few years, which has increased the wealth of the region no end.

* * *

Marie Paz and I talked a while before we went our separate ways to bed. Marie Paz told me that the following morning we were to attend a community meeting, where I was surprised to learn that the members of the half dozen or so villages that made up the community would converge upon the village square. This was news to me, but for some reason, unbeknown to me, I didn't really think much of it.

Marie Paz also asked me, in Spanish of course, how I had slept the night before. I said I had frozen. She said, "How many frazadas do you want?" I said, "I don't know, maybe two or three more," she said, "Ok let's try two more, see if that's enough"; and so Maria Paz gave me a couple more blankets, which would clearly help with the cold. I was then up to nine in total, but I soon discovered that I was still not warm enough.

That night the sand flies returned to feast on my hands, so much so that they woke me again in the early hours, the misbegotten. Sometimes I would awake choking from lack of oxygen; I could only hope that that would improve. I was so cold I unrolled my sleeping bag and slept in it under the blankets, which was some relief. The pot came in handy but getting out of bed in the cold of night in early spring, high in the Peruvian Andes, is not something that I would recommend, unless absolutely necessary.

Sunday 6th September

The following morning, I began the day with my usual Englishman's wash al fresco, in the garden, whilst Cleo Fé chased the cows out of her kitchen and around the garden. Marie Paz chased the chickens away from the breakfast table with a stick, and the dogs lay on the grass beside the table just outside the kitchen door. Juan Carlos arrived to join us for a breakfast of porridge followed by the luxury of eggs and bread rolls.

Marie Paz mentioned that the community were to have a meeting to discuss the matter of the miners, that morning. Such is the way of South America, where there was little warning with regard to the plans of the day.

When Juan Carlos had momentarily disappeared, I asked Marie Paz "What meeting? A miners' meeting? What miners?"

"The miners that want to work here," she said.

"They want to work here?"

"Yes."

"Why do they want to work here?"

"They want to mine for gold."

"What gold?"

"The gold that's in them there hills above the village"

"You mean there's gold in them there hills up above the village?"

"Yes."

"How much?"

"We don't know, but quite a lot"

"You mean Apuquri is literally sitting on a gold mine?" Marie Paz said, "In a manner of speaking yes, and we have to have a meeting because the miners need signatures from everyone in the community for them to have permission to extract the ore." (All of which was spoken in Spanish of course). This meant that the community was living on top of an enormous pile of gold that could be worth hundreds of millions of dollars. This was too incredible to be believed. In theory a village seemingly so poor could soon become very wealthy indeed, this really didn't sink in, so sudden a change was unimaginable.

When we had had enough to eat, at around 10.00 a.m., the three of us, plus Coaser and Cabo, strolled down the steep stony path to attend the community meeting in the village plaza. Not much was said on the way down to town and when we arrived I noticed that Juan Carlos had disappeared, he hadn't said anything; he had quite simply left us without a word.

The morning was idyllic, the sky was clear blue and the majestic peaks of the Andes looked down upon the plaza that was drenched in a glorious bright clear sunshine that is only seen where there is no pollution in the air at all, or if you happen to be skiing.

The concrete terraces on two sides of the plaza were half filled with the people of the community that oversaw a couple of wooden tables situated in the centre of what was normally used as a football pitch. The three main dignitaries, the Alcalde[xxvi] and his two assistants sat at the tables, looking slightly the worse for wear. They were quite often slightly inebriated, and this morning was no exception. That is the way of the administration in rural Peru, and it was not to be frowned upon, as it might be in Europe, even though the politicians' conduct is not entirely dissimilar. To the right on one of the front rows of the concrete seats, separated from the locals were the representatives of the mining company who had come along with their lawyer. They were different in their manner to the locals; they were educated men from the city and were taller and better dressed. They seemed to be particularly seedy; to me they reeked of sleaze.

The community of Apuquri consisted of the main village with a population of around 406, plus six or seven other smaller villages or annexes, some of which were as far as two or three hours walk away, that brought the total population of the community to approximately 700 in number. These villages are some of the highest in Peru at over 4,000 metres above sea level. One called Huayara, two hours' brisk walk from Apuquri has no electricity or running water, where the population of thirty-five retires to bed when the sun goes down and rises when the sun comes up. The people live a very modest life, are incredibly gentle and civil and often live to be over one hundred years old. The cattle walk themselves up the mountain slopes to graze during the day and then return to their respective walled paddocks to spend the night, and partake of a salt lick, all without the direction of a cowherd. The sheep are taken up to graze in the mountain pastures and then they are brought back down again by a well-trained sheep dog, without the aid of a shepherd. The dogs suckle the sheep when they are as yet not weaned, to bond with the herd. The dogs are given food before they leave in the morning and again when they return, in this way they are trained, until they need no shepherd and care for the sheep themselves.

These places are not always idyllic; a young girl of two years old was discovered five years previously, kept in a room all alone. She was born as the consequence of rape, and was dumb and blind at the time. She was kept hidden away because the people of the tiny village were ashamed, they thought she was some sort of divine retribution from God, or Apu Ronco perhaps.

* * *

In the 1950's the government of Peru decreed that the land belonged to the people that worked upon it, which in effect had created a socialist system of land ownership, a fall-back to the laws of the Inca jurisdiction. This meant that rural land became the property of the people, who had no Landlord, and the people began to work together as autonomous communities. The land all around us belonged to the community of Apuquri and the rules dictated that the miners needed first to pay the community an amount of money to investigate the area to see if there were any minerals, in this case gold. Then the miners needed to buy a licence[xxvii] from the state to allow them to extract the minerals. The initial two stages having been completed, the meeting was held in an attempt to obtain the required agreement of all the villagers to extract the copious amounts of gold that had been discovered in the mountains above us.

The community didn't have rights over the gold itself, but the mighty conglomerate did have to gain permission to pass over the land to mine it, which is much the same system of regulation for the extraction of minerals as in most parts of the world. It turned out that the miners would attempt to buy votes by giving bribes such as bottles of frying oil and a few vegetables, whilst others were given the promise of work. Some of the villagers were rewarded if they persuaded those dissenting to change their minds, one of those, it turned out, was Juan Carlos, who was working for the miners.

The people were soon respectfully quiet and the meeting began with the Alcalde's assistant (the Mayor's right hand man) introducing the mining company's representatives followed by the voicing of the company's proposals made one by one. The incentives offered in return for signing over of hundreds of millions of dollars' worth of mining rights consisted of a metalled road all the way up the Cliffside valley to the village, and a bridge, (both of which the miners would need anyway to remove the ore), five computers for the community, a visit from a medic once a month (they didn't say how long for) and a tractor. All of the offers were greeted with an air of nonchalance, but when they got to the offer of the tractor, the crowd became animated. A tractor was something they could really do something with. There was much debate about what make and type of tractor it should be. One woman stood up and said with great pride, as though she was being really clever, as if to say I know what you're like. "You offer us a tractor but is it to be new or second hand?", that produced a murmur of agreement in the crowd and it may have brought about the offer of a new tractor, which I believe was a "John Deere", there are other tractors of course, such as Massey Ferguson or New Holland for example. The miners also said that they would clean up the mess when they finished polluting the environment, which I believe was as likely as a politician telling the truth.

If I were to describe the people of the community, the expression "worldly wise" would not be the first that would spring to mind; they hadn't the faintest clue as to what they could get out of this deal, they had no idea of the potential profit that the miners could make; or how false the promises

72

made could be. This was quite disturbing to say the least. I told Marie Paz to get up and ask for a percentage of the profits, she said, "Can we do that, how much should I ask for?" I said, "I don't know, maybe you should start with 25% and see how it goes, maybe you can get 5 or 10% in the end". So Marie Paz stood up, clearly very nervous and with a little hesitation when asked, she proposed that "The community want the miners to give us a percentage of the profits from the mine". Each one of the miners sat up abruptly and took notice, they suddenly turned their heads towards us in unison, as though in an old black and white Laurel and Hardy movie. The Alcalde then addressed Marie Paz very calmly. "What? He said. You want a percentage of the profits and how much should we ask for?" Marie Paz said, with unmistakeable clarity "We want 50%", I thought "You go Marie Paz"; nonetheless, though a good place to start, 50% was possibly quite a lot to ask. The miners looked at us in disbelief, their exploitation may well have been in jeopardy; whilst almost every one of those campesinos looked completely bewildered. I could almost hear them saying "What is a percentage? Profits? Is anyone making profits? What profits?" Clearly the gold had no value in comparison to food, and they were more interested in the tractor, because they could use that to improve the crops and build things. Those poor uneducated campesinos didn't appear to understand the machinations of the situation; and so the proposal was noted, but it did seem that it was virtually brushed aside as an irrelevant memo to the agenda. Nonetheless, thankfully, I may well have been wrong.

Shortly before the end of the meeting a second mining company, until then unnoticed, also offered a proposal to undertake a survey on the other side of the valley. That was noted, but was also virtually brushed aside; there was definitely gold in the hills above us, and tons of it. The community of Apuquri was literally sitting on a mountain of money, but they had no idea of what to do with the power beneath their fingertips.

As the assembly drew to a close the mining officials walked up to the central table and signed something, my heart rate rose to fever pitch. I called to Marie Paz "No están firmando un contrato? Es imprescindible que no lo firmen" or "They are not signing the contract are they? It's imperative that they don't sign". I'm sure Marie Paz saw the panic in my eyes when she reassured me. I felt a whole lot better when she told me that they were merely signing the "asistencia" or minutes of the meeting. She said that the outlying villages didn't want to sign, they didn't want the upheaval and the contamination, and they didn't like or trust the mining companies. They had no desire to have the tranquillity of their lives destroyed by the intervention of the miners, or indeed money. They had no real desire to become wealthy; the spondulicks would, no doubt, cause nothing but destruction.

As the meeting was drawing to an end, Marie Paz told me that the community leaders had agreed to meet the miners on the following Wednesday. I explained to Marie Paz that it was crucial that the community organise a private meeting beforehand to establish a united front to present to the miners; the village committee was planning to turn up and discuss everything openly, without any prior assembly, which was commercial suicide. Up until that time they had not had meetings to prepare for negotiation with the miners, which to me was madness. I later learned that the proposed meeting with the miners never came to fruition.

While the people began to go their separate ways, the few mining directors and their lawyer walked over to us to introduce themselves to Marie Paz and myself; each one of them greeted us and shook our hands in turn. They were incredibly polite and courteous, they were particularly curious about my presence, but we were not overly forthcoming. We just mentioned that I was helping out with a charity project. They were ingratiating in their manner, unctuous in fact, in a style not entirely dissimilar in texture to the cooking oil they used to offer as a bribe; I didn't trust them at all.

* * *

The mining directors walked on and Marie Paz and I walked up through the village past the church into one of the streets near not too far up from the building project, where we had celebrated the forthcoming sembrada[xxviii] and had blessed Pachamama the previous day, with a few drinks. There were a few women weaving brightly coloured cloth at the side of the street; something that was not often seen in Apuquri.

We had found ourselves in a slight predicament; the building was about 750 adobe bricks short of the full Monty. We needed to make arrangement for them to be made, and to pay for them. Juan Carlos should have been arranging the deal but surprisingly he was nowhere to be seen. It was normal for a man to do such things, so Marie Paz was grateful of any charitable weight that I may have carried, at the time I wasn't exactly sure why. I thought this was slightly unfounded, though I was wrong. I have no idea why, but a man, such as myself, seemed to make some impression without doing very much at all.[xxix]

We soon discovered our contractual adobe-making friend, following a few enquiries; he was sitting in the street outside a friend's house. The greeting for the meeting was quite methodical in its way, in the manner of any other business deal. Following the formalities and the agreement of the price, my job was to go and buy a couple of large bottles of beer, which we all shared, to seal the deal.

I didn't understand everything that was said at that time by any stretch of the imagination. The spoken Spanish had a strong accent and it was interspersed with some Quechua; that's my excuse anyway. When they were discussing the making of the bricks they spoke a particular prescribed language, using incredibly respectful terminology. It was not entirely dissimilar to a business meeting anywhere in the Western World, except that they referred to each other as "maestro" or "my respectful friend" and we were standing in dust-ridden street, not in a boardroom. We arranged for the adobe bricks to be made for quite a lot of money in relative terms, Sol. 750 or £150, whichever was easier. Marie Paz made a few notes on a piece of paper, which was to be the contract; and when the beer was drunk and the contract was signed, we said our farewells and walked back up the hill to the house. There was no further discussion, the deal was done, and there was no complication thereafter.

When we arrived at the steps at the front of the house we were met by Victor and a couple of his mates. Victor was a forthright man, one of the few who had spoken out at the meeting; he had voiced his disapproval of the miners which was not normal for a paisano;[xxx] mainly because the majority were afraid to speak out, they were overwhelmed by the power that the miners represented.

Whilst Marie Paz graciously retired to make supper, I was honoured with an invitation into the shop opposite for a drink. The four of us sat in an unlit corner, at a dusty wooden table, whilst the young lady behind the counter came to serve us a couple of bottles of beer and a few shots of the local hooch. I gave them a couple of rollups, made from Golden Virginia tobacco (There are other tobaccos) which they thought was marvellous. They had never seen tobacco rolled, or indeed sold, from Europe before. Marie Paz later told me it was an experience that they would tell all of their friends.

As we talked it soon became apparent that it was difficult to resist the pressure from the miners and it was dangerous to speak out against them. I hadn't realised at the time quite how perilous it was. They were in the process of explaining to me that I had better not talk openly against the miners, when Juan Carlos suddenly arrived, from where I do not know. We hadn't seen him since early that morning. Marie Paz must have told him where we were. When he sat down Juan Carlos told me, in no uncertain terms, that members of the charity were not supposed to get involved in political matters and that I shouldn't discuss the proposed mining contract, which was ironic, I later discovered. I said that was fine of course, but surely it was not a problem if I wanted to voice an opinion in private over a few beers? He said that that should not cause any difficulty, but that I really shouldn't get too involved. In fact what Juan Carlos meant was that the subject was best avoided altogether.

In the UK we don't worry about speaking out on political matters. It is easy to forget that overseas, things are a lot different. Also when there are potentially millions upon millions of dollars involved, for example in mining gold, people can get a little anxious, especially in a place miles from anywhere, in a village, high in the mountains, where there were no police at all. It was becoming more and more apparent that the miners were extremely influential and no doubt they also had friends in even higher places, who might not take too kindly to anyone who had the potential to interfere with their enterprise.

We carried on drinking, passing around one glass, until after an hour or so, the shop had ran out of beer, so we all went our separate ways. Juan Carlos and I walked down the street, where we tapped on the window of what seemed to be an ordinary adobe house, with only a miniscule sign on the wall outside. A lady with many skirts came to the tiny window eventually and let us in. As was often the custom it was the family's front room that was used as a convenience store. It may have been dark and dusty with an obligatory earthen floor, but they did have beer, so I bought a couple more.

We went back to Marie Paz's where she had made us something to eat. We didn't discuss anything in particular during the meal and after a couple more drinks Juan Visconti left to go home. When he had gone Marie Paz told me to be careful of what I said in front of Juan Carlos. The miners sometimes came to stay in the village, in a house that they had bought in the centre of town just off the main plaza. This house looked slightly less unkempt than the other houses and was often empty. She told me that the miners often gave Juan Carlos a lift downtown to Chalhuanca, in one of their 4 x 4's, that were seen from time to time in the village. It was rumoured that Juan Carlos had been trying to persuade the locals to sign away their rights on behalf of the miners, Marie

Paz supposed for some kind of payment of very little at all. It rapidly became apparent that Juan Carlos was not all that he appeared to be.

* * *

I learned that Marie Paz had spent her formative years with an order of nuns named "Las Hermanas de la Caridad Dominicas de la Presentación de la Santisima Virgen". She went to live with them initially in Lima, Peru, when she was sixteen years old. Later she was transferred to spend her time caring for the children in the most poverty stricken areas of Medellin, Colombia, where she lived for three years. After that she spent several years living with the tribe Los Trinitarios, in the region of Chapari in the Bolivian jungle, in what is the poorest country in South America,[xxxi] yet a beautiful place.

Later, in the early 1990's, Marie Paz, went to work in a town in southern Peru near Lake Titicaca; a place where the terrorist faction the "Sendero Luminoso" or "Shining Path", were known to seek refuge in the convents. A Maoist movement, the Sendero Luminoso wanted to eradicate corruption within the authorities in Peru, with the ultimate motivation to establish a communist state. The leader, Ibamael Guzmán, launched his campaign against the state in 1980, from the region of Ayacucho. This was largely ignored by the armed forces at the outset; mainly because the insurgence was in general related to land redistribution within the rural areas of the Andes which were and are populated mainly by indigenous Amerindian groups and therefore largely distant from the government radar.

Sunday 6th September

In some areas the military trained "Rondas Campesinas", who were groups originally created by the peasants to make a stand against theft, and in particular cattle rustling. However they were later formed to act against the revolutionary Sendero Luminoso. The Rondas were generally poorly equipped, despite being supported by the state. The first reported attack by the Rondas, was in January 1983, near Huata, Ayacucho, when it was reported that thirteen "Senderistas" were killed.

It is further reported that in March 1983 in Lucanamarca, a small town in the Huanca Sancos region of Ayacucho, the Rondas had brutally killed a Sendero Luminoso commander named Oligaro Curitomay. They took him to the town square, stoned him, stabbed him, set him on fire and finally shot him. In retaliation it is reported that the Sendero Luminoso massacred 69 people, including eighteen children, the youngest being only six months old; eleven women, some of whom were pregnant and eight people who were between fifty and seventy years old.

It is said that most of the victims were hacked to death by machetes and axes, while many of the others were shot at close range. It was also rumoured that other villagers were scalded with boiling water as a punishment. This was known as the "Massacre of Lucanamarca", the first killings within the peasant community by the Sendero Luminoso. The event was supposedly admitted by the leader Abimael Guzmán, in an interview with El Diario, a pro-shining-path newspaper based in Lima. Guzmán explained the rationale as that "In the face of military actions .... we responded with devastating action." "The main point being to make them understand that we were a hard nut to crack, and that we were

80

ready for anything, anything." There are other nuts available, of course.

There were several other massacres reportedly committed by the Sendero Luminoso thereafter, including one in Haullo, Tambo District, which is said to have ended with the death of 47, including fourteen children aged between four and fifteen years.

The army were involved in the training the Rondas Campesinas and were also known to commit atrocities at that time. Many innocent people were known to have been arrested by the authorities and detained under suspicion of being members of the terrorist faction, but these are unreported. The question arises therefore as to how accurate and to what extent the information published by the media was manipulated by those in power and it is not unreasonable to suggest that the official reports of the actions of the Sendero Luminoso may not be entirely authentic. The killing of women and children does not comply with the beliefs of the terrorists.

The Sendero Luminoso were known to infiltrate society by using fear tactics. They would summon communities to meetings declaring that if you weren't with them, you were against them, and rejection of their regime could mean forced labour or death. In reality this was an enterprise not entirely dissimilar to that of the Spanish Inquisition. Ordinary members of society were used to inform on political figures, or people in authority such as democratically elected officials who were suspected of corruption; the Sendero Luminoso would find the perpetrators and kill them. However, I was told by the son of a senior member of the army, for example, that there was a knock on his father's door one morning, and he was advised not to go to the office. A bomb attack ensued on the very same military establishment. Why did the Senderistas warn such a senior member of the army? They did so because they did not believe that he was corrupt.

The Sendero Luminoso controlled much of the central and southern Andean highlands in the 1980's. The Senderistas bombed Lima many times and killed and injured many people. It is understood that more than 69,000 people died as a consequence of a conflict that in many ways was a civil war. It appears that the motive of the Sendero Luminoso was ultimately to eradicate corruption within the Peruvian authorities, but it is unlikely that the truth will ever be known. The image portrayed by the media was one of indiscriminate violence, and it is likely that that may have not been entirely true, fear is after all, always a useful tool of manipulation.

The Sendero Luminoso were most active from 1980 until the capture of their leader Abimael Guzmán in 1992; since that time their operations have declined enormously. Though in 2012 they are known to have been attempting to revive their infiltration of society in the Apurimac Region North of Cuzco. The president has activated a zero tolerance attitude and troops have been sent to the region to quell any possible resurgence of terrorist activity, if they can be found.

* * *

Towards the end of the peak of Sendero Luminoso activity, in the early 1990's, Marie Paz was living close to Lake Titicaca. She was caring for the poor children in the region with a couple of sisters from Colombia. It is said that one day in the springtime, representatives of the Sendero

Luminoso called all of the members of the community in which they were living, to a meeting. This was an invitation that was difficult to refuse unless you were a Colombian nun, and not a Peruvian national. This left Marie Paz to take the children to the gathering in the central plaza, where the Alcalde and his five or so assistant members of the council were seated at the front of the crowded plaza in an elevated position. What ensued was quite horrific. The Senderistas began to accuse each council member in turn, of corruption, abuse of power, drunkenness, and possible fornication; and for those reasons they were shot in the head at close range, on the stage, in front of the whole of the community, including all the women and children.

Unsurprisingly, the sight of those bloody murders disturbed Marie Paz deeply, so much so in fact, that she began to suffer heart palpitations and became quite unwell. These events affected her so badly that she left the Sisters of Dominica and returned to live with her mother in Lima, at around thirty one years of age. This led Marie Paz to other charitable endeavours, which moved her to work in the orphanage funded from the UK, where I had stayed in Lima.

It then came about that the same charity that ran the orphanage in Lima had organised funds for the construction of the Casa Hogar in Apuquri, of which I was to support. Marie Paz had volunteered to supervise the works but Carolina, the head of the orphanage, had told her that the charity couldn't afford to pay a supervisor. So Marie Paz had resigned from the orphanage to come back to her roots, to oversee the construction, to set up and run the Casa Hogar, without a wage. This work was her vocation in life. She could only afford to do this because she knew that she would have the full support of the community.

I was shocked to learn, that when Marie Paz arrived back in Apuquri, she had discovered that Juan Carlos, Carolina's husband, had been employed by the charity to run the construction of the Casa Hogar for a salary, the very same salary that they had said that they couldn't afford to pay Marie Paz. It was not therefore entirely surprising that Juan Carlos had not been offered a room in Marie Paz's house.

I was also surprised to learn that two nuns from the same Dominican order, had been sacked from the orphanage in Lima where Marie Paz had been working, and where I had stayed. No explanation was given as to the reason for their ejection. We could only suspect, that perhaps there were certain aspects of the orphanage, that certain people did not want reported to what is an incredibly powerful institution in South America, namely the Dominican Order.

* * *

As mentioned before, the initial works, being the construction of the concrete footings for the Casa Hogar, had been undertaken predominantly by a team of volunteers from the RAF, who had travelled all the way from England for a few weeks to support the project. It then transpired that upon the completion of the footings, the RAF team had left early in disgust due to the frequent absence of Juan Carlos and Marie Paz had been left to pick up the pieces. Despite all of that, Juan Carlos was still present, but clearly only on occasion, in his official capacity as the managing director of the project. He was supposed to get his hands dirty when he had time, but that was a rare occurrence, and he could not be criticised for his lacking in that. His main occupation was after all as manager, to order materials when needed, but apparently this did not include adobe bricks. Clearly there was more to the internal politics of this construction project than met the eye, all was not as it had seemed.

Juan Carlos suffered no retribution for his conduct. The workers were so naïve that they thought that it took a long time to order materials, days in fact. This was verified when John Visconti (AKA Hercules) quantified the fact. He told me that he thought it must take an awful lot of work in order to obtain the same. I didn't put him right of course; I didn't want to upset the apple cart. I suppose it was merely the way of the world, a man in a managerial position, who is not under supervision, will do as he pleases, and the locals were none the wiser.

I also learned that Juan Carlos was also from a family that had at one time been in possession of some not inconsiderable amount of money derived from certain mining projects; from his family history it was clear where his loyalty would ultimately lie. There is a social hierarchy in Peru and the campesinos are not considered as being at the top of the pile. Juan Carlos was simply aspiring to those that had power within the social strata. This put Juan Carlos, in a sense, at the lowest ethical echelon himself; such are the trials and tribulations of the merchant classes.

* * *

That night, it was cold, I said to Marie Paz I needed more blankets, she said, "Cuantos necesitas?" I said, "Dos más debe ser suficiente" she said, "¿Seguro?" I said, "Si, seguro, gracias" and I was given a couple more blankets. I was now up to eleven, which finally seemed to work. I was no longer waking up from the cold. I only awoke from choking through lack of oxygen or from the painful itching of the sand fly bites on my hands. Note to self "Buy some insect repellent when next in town."

Monday 7th September

Marie Paz and I got up early to go to Chalhuanca to buy some food. After breakfast we walked downtown at about 8.00 a.m. with the dogs. Coaser had disappeared and a very friendly amusing dog known as Saltarin[xxxii] had turned up to take his place. Along the way into town Saltarin and Cabo took great pleasure in growling at several other dogs as we passed by. We found a taxi and asked if they were going to Chalhuanca, the driver said no, then called us back to say that the cab was full, which didn't really make sense. We then found another cab which was also full; it was a dark blue Japanese estate car with four on the back seat and two in the boot. Marie Paz sat in the back and they put me in the front, because I suppose, I was the biggest. The taxi drove for 45 minutes or so down the gravel track and fifteen or so minutes along the Pan-American Highway into the urban centre that is Chalhuanca, for the princely sum of Sol. 5 (£1.00) per person.

Marie Paz and I had been discussing the possibility of buying seeds for the community so when we arrived in town Marie Paz tried to call a contact who may have been able to find us some Quinoa, but we had no luck. Sadly that was the only time we attempted to procure seeds. I didn't want to interfere too much in the pride of the community and the subject was soon forgotten, but we did try, albeit only briefly.

Our main motivation for the shopping trip was to buy provisions, so we then went to the large covered market that sunk down and sat above the rocky outcrop on the river's edge, just behind the main square. This type of permanent indoor market place, made up of individual stall holders, is a type of market that can be found in almost every town in Peru. This particular one was situated on two floors with very high ceilings. The whitewashed walls gave the place a relatively refreshing, bright and airy atmosphere. They sold fresh fish, organic meat, fruit, vegetables and pulses of various types; but I noticed not too many spices. These markets are used as a meeting place where you can also buy a meal, a hot drink or fruit juice. There are several stalls where you can sit at the bar and eat from one of the set menus at any time of the day for a very reasonable price. Although to the European it may seem a little rustic, and health and safety wouldn't be happy, the food is incredibly wholesome and fresh. What I like about these markets is that they are very sociable places, the food on sale is in effect organic and in this one the fish was more often than not taken from the river Apurimac that ran just below the market itself.

Marie Paz ordered the rice, potatoes and other vegetables that she wanted, we then walked back past the street vendors in the plaza. They sold all manner of things such as bric-a-brac, homemade bread and cheese, various types of cold drinks, local meat kebabs and live chicks that needed to be home grown. We walked across the plaza onto the main street to one of the many stores, where Marie Paz knew the staff. We were in search of a chicken and a few other provisions.

We stepped down into a store where the shelves were stacked full of all manner of bottles and tins of various products. There were several types of locally caught fish in the fridge and a pile of plucked chickens with their heads still on, lying on a table to one side adjacent to the counter, looking at me. Cleanliness did not appear to be high on the agenda, there were a few flies buzzing around the place, but no one seemed to give a monkey's. The shopkeeper was chopping up fresh trout on a very bloody chopping board behind the counter. Marie Paz chose a chicken and asked the shopkeeper to chop it up. There appear to be very few people in Peru who fillet a chicken as they do in Europe, we all too easily forget that that is a skill. That day was no exception; the assistant wiped the remnants of fish from the blood soaked slab with a grubby old cloth, and slapped the chicken onto the work surface that elsewhere might be considered as positively dangerous, because, no doubt, a plethora of bacteria lived quite happily. He then proceeded to hack the chicken into rough pieces and throw them into a dodgy old plastic carrier bag that he had picked up from off the floor.

I think if that had happened in Tesco's, (there are other supermarkets) Health and Safety would have had a field day; that is if they had got past the front door of the shop. There would have been numerous complaints, someone would have fainted and the store would have been closed down; probably by an Armed Special Response Police Unit with helicopters, ambulances and a specially trained Hostage Recovery Team which included a professional negotiator and sniffer dogs.

If eaten by your average sanitized 21st Century computer geek, that meat would be very likely to cause some terrible stomach problem, a viral infection or even death; which is not entirely unlike the insidious destruction caused by fast food, microwaves and over sanitation. This, however, was not the case in Chalhuanca, or Apuquri for that matter, where they must have been doing something right. It seems that less sanitation creates a longer life, the people in the region often live to complete a century. There was no ant-bacterial hand wash, no sanitary wipes, no "now wash your hands signs", no vacuum cleaners, no neurotic people telling you how to conduct your own personal hygiene, no OCD, no Attention Deficit Disorder, no antidepressants, no plastic surgery, no plastic people, and no panic.

* * *

When we had bought all the necessary provisions, we had a very good wholesome lunch together, probably of Llama steak and chips, in a restaurant frequented by miners. This meant that it was better that we didn't talk about anything to do with the exploitation at the miner's meeting of the previous day, in case it may be overheard. The miners have a strong, powerful presence in Chalhuanca; they are a separate race that could be seen driving around in their 4 x 4's, overlooking the manor.

Apuquri had one computer apparently, though I hadn't seen it yet, mainly because it was only on rare occasions that it might actually work. So, after the meal, I took the opportunity to spend about half an hour in an internet café down one of the side streets. In comparison to the rest of life in the mountains, sitting on the computer was as always uneventful, and extremely dull and frustrating, but I did manage to send some messages back home, and someone had sent me a link, which was nice.

Marie Paz went off somewhere for half an hour and then came into the café to find me. She waited a short time for me to finish my emails, to which my girlfriend was not still being entirely forthcoming, she was not happy with me at all.

This would no doubt have had something to do with female logic, which I have never understood and probably never will; in common with the rest of male gender since time immemorial, being 6 July 1189, the date of the inauguration of King Richard I. Sadly, I would not recommend a trip to South America to maintain a good relationship.

We did a little more shopping around town until it was time for our return journey. As arranged we found the same taxi waiting in the same main street, to take us back at 4.00 p.m. The fare had gone up, because the taxi had to go up, and that would use more petrol, which is logical I suppose. The car filled up, to go up, with about six more passengers. I was sat up front and we each paid our Sol. 6 up front, the driver needed the money to fill up with petrol up front, just out of town; then we drove out of town along the metalled road and then up the old mountain track into Apuquri with the obligatory Peruvian music, crackling on the radio.

As we drove, darkness was beginning to fall, and there was a chill in the air. When we finally arrived at home Marie Paz and I had a couple of drinks and a very good supper, and then an early night, in bed at around 9.00 p.m., after watching a couple of incredibly dull chat shows with Peruvian intellectuals, in the background, on one of the two available TV channels. One of them was an uncanny Peruvian Stephen Fry look-a-like.

That evening, Marie Paz told me a little of the miners exploitation of the people, and their search for gold. She told me how the naïve innocence of some of the mountain communities had led them to sign over their rights for virtually nothing.

The mining was a double-edged sword, the mines themselves are an eyesore; when the gold is extracted the water table becomes polluted and also that which surrounds it. Apparently a lot of waste had in fact, already harmed the Apurimac River, which was a valuable source of trout, and other fish. Primarily the implications of the environmental damage are obvious, but secondly the mines may destroy a way of life that is centuries old. If the campesinos do gain money from these projects it will enable them to buy their way into the 21st Century and everything that comes with it. This would mean that it will no longer be necessary for the communities to work together to cultivate and harvest the cákras in the traditional way. The sense of community would dissipate as the onset of technology would enable the people to live more solitary lonely lives sitting in front of a computer screen. Ultimately the invasion of the modernity of the 21st Century would destroy a way of life. This was a way of life which seems to be so much healthier than the self-destructive, computerised, urban lifestyles of most of the so called, sophisticated technological societies of today.

Marie Paz also told me something that quite unnerved me. A mountain community, in one of the valleys nearby, had signed over their mining rights and consequently the miners had begun their work. The presence of the miners is an incursion; they take over everything in their 4 x 4's, as though a foreign army of men have invaded. In that valley close by there was a man, a schoolteacher, who had become more and more outspoken against the mining company, and the mining company weren't very happy about what he was saying. The teacher was constantly voicing his opinion in public and was stirring up some discontent amongst the local inhabitants.

That was until one day that teacher was travelling in a people carrier,[xxxiii] when there was a minor collision with the side of the road which was sufficiently serious for the emergency services to have been called, such as they were. Some people suffered minor bruising, but nothing serious and everyone seemed to have survived with little more than a scratch and a few bruises. That was until they discovered that the teacher had disappeared. He was eventually discovered two weeks later, face down in a river nearby, and little was done to find out who was responsible.

I awoke that night at round 11.00 p.m., not from the cold, I now had eleven blankets, nor from the sand flies, I now had insect repellent, nor from oxygen starvation, but from the realisation that I could be considered a problem for the miners. I was painfully aware that they must have known that I had the ability to stir up some trouble. This meant that in theory I could cost the miners millions of dollars and it would therefore be better if I were out of the way. Juan Carlos was in bed[xxxiv] with the miners who had seen me at the meeting. I didn't know what Juan Carlos had told them about me, or for that matter if he'd told them where I was living.

I had made a fuss at the meeting on Sunday morning and had foolishly talked quite openly against the miners in the bar on that evening; at the time I had no idea that Juan Carlos was a friend of the miners. It became all too apparent that I was considerably more transparent in my opinion than I should have been. I became incredibly aware that I was in a foreign country miles from normal civilisation and the nearest police were at least an hour away by car. What was of some additional concern was that even if there were any police presence, (without wishing to denigrate the Peruvian Police Force) they could probably be bought off anyway, the miners simply had too much power and were clearly, potentially very dangerous.

Surprising as it may seem, whilst I mulled these ideas over in my mind, in the inky blackness of that night, in the freezing cold of my bedroom, I wasn't altogether comfortable and every sound became acute, I couldn't sleep for quite some time. My mind had suddenly become very clear; it was no longer so clouded by the initial culture shock of South America. I realised the clear and present danger of my situation and became very concerned for my own safety. I resolved from then on to be extremely careful about anything that I may say in relation to the gold in the hills above us; I had no intention of ending my days face down in a river. I finally got to sleep sometime after 5.00 a.m.

Tuesday 8th September

I got up at 7.30 a.m., it was a beautiful sun shiny day. I had a quick wash, got dressed for work, in shorts, foolishly it turned out. I soon learned that the sand flies were not only active at night. Following breakfast Marie Paz and I walked down the steep incline of the path to the building site, with Cabo and Saltarin of course (Coaser had disappeared). There were six of us at work that day, Constantino, (the 85 year old man with the walking stick,) was mixing mud for the adobe bricks, as usual in bare feet, with his trousers rolled up to his knees. Four guys (Don Fernando, Roger, Peso and Sebas) were loading out and laying the bricks. John Visconti (AKA Hercules) and I had the job of levelling the floors of the rooms. This work, no task for the faint hearted, involved moving a couple of tons of dry earth and rocks, not to mention quite a few fallen adobe bricks. It was a hot day and we got to work to lower the ground level to the top of the concrete foundations at the base of the walls. The walls were less than a metre high, set out (obviously) as the base of what was to become a rather large Casa Hogar that would be big enough to sleep more than thirty children. It was hard work in the heat and the air was taxing as was normal at that altitude; for myself it would take a while to become accustomed to that labour.

Although the language was the same Spanish interspersed with Quechua, it rapidly became apparent that they were all making fun of Hercules. They called him Hercules because, although very strong, he was extremely skinny. They also called him "Maricón" and they told me to be careful because he liked men, the reason being that he didn't have a girlfriend and he lived with his mother. It was the same sense of humour as if I were working on a building site in England, every joke was told with a straight face, well at least most of the time. The humour had not become infested with Political Correctness, they were very funny and all was taken in the good humour in which it was intended.

We could also work without a shirt, we could wear shorts and no one would sue for a melanoma, even if they knew what one was. The muck was also mixed barefoot, so no work-safety-boots, but there were helmets, however I only ever saw a photo of them. No one was driven crazy by rules that make no sense at all, there was no Health and Safety, and there was no madness.

Sadly for the modern world, Health and Safety officers normally have little or no experience of the profession that they are employed to monitor. Consequently they may intervene when one is least expecting it. Rather than stay at home listening to the radio, they must ensure that they are seen to be doing something. That is why a carpenter may have to wear a high-viz jacket or a roof-tiler will have to wear long trousers at all times. Nowadays it is illegal in the UK for a hodcarrier to carry a hod of bricks up a ladder, and that trade is as old as the houses themselves.

So I found it unbelievably refreshing to work in that place, without luminous clothing or fear of intervention. I was far from the madding crowd, where the jokes ran rife and no one would accuse you of being drunk for saying "Indians", instead of "Native Americans". There was a lot of common sense, but there were no high-viz jackets, no one bothered to wear a safety helmet and the job I was doing was perfectly legal. There was no Health and Safety, there was no PC, there were no mephitic Human Resources to contaminate our lives in the mountains, and there was no win no fee.

* * *

Two incredibly harmful virulent strains of virus have infected the modern world over recent years, and they are difficult to escape. They have crept into all walks of life and they are out of control, they have become so prevalent that they are almost impossible to eradicate. They have, over time, developed complete immunity against any form of common sensibility. Western Society has become infested with Political Correctness and Health and Safety, and as yet there is no known cure.

Initially nobody realised exactly how much unrest they were creating in the workplace and there were attempts by personnel to keep them in check, but they have had very limited success. They themselves became defiled by the same contagion, and those within it became malevolent, depraved, nefarious, loathsome individuals who rather than control the plague, have increased the malignant growth.

Personnel have now become so infected that they have now become probably what can only be described as possibly the greatest threat to humanity as we know it........ many people have heard of this menace but few understand them or are aware of quite what they are capable of. They have become more dangerous than were the Nazis, the Communist Regime, the IRA or ETA, they are a greater menace than the Sendero Luminoso or other extremist factions. This noxious body of human remnants have become an entity known as......... as, as, Human Resources; so be afraid, be very afraid and never, ever, forget to lock your doors at night.

All may not be lost, there may be hope in sight, there may be light on the horizon. There are certain individuals, who will remain nameless for their own protection, who have set about the creation of new laws. These are consequent upon "Parkinson's theory at work" which states that work expands to fill the time available for its completion and that the number of administrators in an office is bound to increase over time. If these laws are to become a reality, they will provide punishment for those found to have been practicing unnecessary Health and Safety or overactive Political Correctness or HR. These penalties should be detention at Her Majesty's pleasure, for a term of not less than 25 years, with a maximum of life.

* * *

Whilst we were working Hercules told me his family were originally of Italian extraction. Ironically they had gone to Apuquri, many years beforehand, in search of gold. They hadn't found any but now someone else had. One of Hercules' Uncles had actually been mayor of the community and I thought that his family might make a claim to it, they were one of the first to arrive after all. It turned out that Hercules had previously been working for himself as a Currency Exchanger in the centre of Lima, for which he had developed a float of some US$27,000.00, or just a small amount of gold. I got the impression that he had been working at the front of one of the larger hotels because he had a smattering of Japanese, he also knew a small amount of English and German. Sadly, one day a few years beforehand, Hercules had been mugged in the street. The perpetrators had stolen all of his money, so he had decided to return home to Apuquri, as he had, in effect, lost the tools of his trade. He once said to me, with a certain sadness in his eyes, "What good is gold or silver if there is no food to eat?" A fair point I think.

* * *

When we spoke about the miners, Hercules told me that the community would never win against them. He was resigned to the expectation that the community would lose; I felt obliged to tell him that that was not entirely true. The rights to the gold belonged to the community and the community could become quite comfortable in consequence. There could be more than enough money to build a new school, to provide health care and to improve the harvests, and even enough to replace the tin (or Calamina) on the church roof with terracotta tiles. Therefore nothing should be signed until a proper contract was agreed with the mining companies. It was sad to learn from Marie Paz later, that there was a rumour that Hercules had already signed away his voting rights for a bottle of cooking oil and a box of vegetables; such is the poverty of Apuquri.

When we broke for lunch at around 12.30 p.m., Hercules and I walked up the hill, in my case quite slowly because I was still unaccustomed to the thin air. I would get out of breath after a few steps, but for Hercules, who was 45, it was no problem at all, he was up and down that slope like a mountain goat. When we arrived chez Marie Paz, after a good ten minutes of chatting, Hercules walked on and I went in to have a fabulous lunch that Marie Paz had prepared a herbal chicken broth, followed by sausages (a rare commodity in Peru) and a little beef with rice and potatoes; it was delicious. The meal was all made in a kitchen that most Europeans would baulk at, and for which, Health and Safety would have put Marie Paz in jail. The ceiling was blackened from the smoke and Guinea Pigs ran around the earthen floor in the hope of any peelings that were deliberately dropped when cooking.

Whilst we ate Marie Paz told me that I was invited to lunch the next day at a friend of hers called Rebecca, who I had met briefly at the miner's meeting. Rebecca was vehemently against the miners. I told Marie Paz I would like to go, but I thought I should work and wasn't sure I should. She said that it was not a problem for me to have the day off, but I wasn't so sure. After lunch I wanted to get back to work but was feeling exhausted; the thin air was getting to me yet again, so I had a sleep for ten minutes before I could return to my labour. Marie Paz really didn't mind at all.

From where the site was, on the edge of a slope halfway up the valley, the view of the surrounding peaks was spectacular. The sky was clear and open that day, but late in the afternoon, shortly before 5 o'clock, we could see clouds moving towards the peaks above us, when they passed over the mountain tops they left a dusting of snow, it was a beautiful sight to see. The clouds continued towards us, lightning began to strike, spectacular thunder rumbled in the distance and heavy drops of rain began to fall upon us. We cleared up very quickly and we all left the site fairly rapidly. Hercules and I ran to shelter as best we could, by an external adobe wall of one of a group of nearby houses. I have to say I was quite nervous as the storm drifted over us. I wasn't used to violent thunderstorms passing over my head at such a high altitude where lightning could easily strike, but Hercules and the others were not fazed at all. I later learned that people had been known to have been struck by, and killed by lightning, but generally in higher, more exposed, climbs.

We waited for about ten minutes until the storm had moved on, then we walked up through the centre of the village to ascend the pathway once more where we met Marie Paz who was on the way down; she was so kind that she was bringing me a waterproof jacket, because of the rain.

Although it was exhausting, (probably due to the lack of oxygen, as much as anything else) I thoroughly enjoyed working on that site, shifting earth with Hercules. The men were making jokes all day long; there was something wholesome and literally down to earth about our labours, which made the working day an absolute pleasure.

The men didn't ask too many questions of me during the day, however they were quite curious about where I came from, they wanted to know about Europe and how long it took to get to Peru and then to Apuquri from Lima, which I told them was more than forty hours travel in total.

They were also curious about my boots, they wondered if they could get some. I was too embarrassed to tell them how much they cost, though I probably just avoided the question. I merely told them that they were expensive. They had cost more than one hundred pounds in England, which was a month's wages for these guys, and I wasn't about to tell them that. Hence the reason why, later on, I tried to find some rubber sandals, made from car tyres, which the men wore. They were like flip flops with two rubber straps crossed at the front, they cost Sol. 5 a pair, but I couldn't find any in my size, which was a shame as I would have liked to be more immersed as one of the workers.

I asked them if I should go to lunch in Puka Wasi[xxxv] with Rebecca the following day; and they told me in no uncertain terms, that I had to go or she would be deeply offended. They didn't mind at all that I would miss the day at work.

Those men may have had very little but they were all good company and happy in their work. We really had a good time; it had been a beautiful almost surreal day working in the Andes.

* * *

When we got back to the house Marie Paz realised that she had left the key to the kitchen locked inside the kitchen, probably not the best place to leave it. So I found a rake and managed to hook the key and bring it out through the window, which was fortunate, I didn't feel like breaking the door down. Marie Paz had prepared yet another fabulous meal, with tuna and vegetables and rice. We ate outside looking down over the lights of the village, with the stars glistening above us and the sound of the dogs barking and fighting in the streets. Sometimes we would hear traditional Peruvian music murmuring beneath us.

When Marie Paz cooked she used a lot of fresh herbs; the meals consisted mainly of rice, potatoes, vegetables and some eggs on occasion. Meat was used sparingly, almost as a flavouring. Any meat had value and was stretched to last; this had a good effect on the digestive system as the stomach was never weighed down, and I had begun to lose weight.

After we had eaten we both walked out across the road where I got some money back on a couple of beer bottles from the shop opposite. We then took the remains, being most of the chicken, to Marie Paz's friend's house down the street to put it in one of the few fridges in town. Marie Paz's friend was a teacher who lived in what we would regard in Europe as abject poverty, but she seemed to be very happy and was very pleased to help us out.

It became more and more apparent that the people in this poverty stricken place were incredibly civilised. As was normal whenever we passed anyone in the street we were received with an incredibly polite greeting; it's a shame we don't act more like that at home, it creates a good feeling within the soul.

We got back at around 8.00 p.m. and we partook in a couple of glasses of the local white rum, cañazo. I told Marie Paz of my concerns of the dangers of the mining company and how I could help with the negotiations of the contract. I didn't want to see those poor campesinos exploited in such an appalling way. It was obvious that even with a small percentage of the profits, the wealth of the community could be improved enormously. What was of equal concern was that the construction of the mining infrastructure had already started, high in the valleys above us. This work had begun with no regard to any agreement, quite simply because there wasn't one, and therefore any work that was on-going was in fact illegal, but they carried on regardless.

When we spoke about any danger that I may have been in Marie Paz assured me that I was quite safe. She told me that the community would protect me which made me feel a whole lot better, but not entirely secure. She also warned me not to speak out, to keep a low profile and avoid discussion on the matter; not least because some members of the community had already been bought, I might add for very little indeed.

Marie Paz went to bed and I stayed up for a while watching the Peruvian TV where I saw the spitting image of Steven Fry again, interviewing politicians in a high brow TV show. I must have got to bed at around midnight.

That night my sleep was much improved, I had eleven blankets and insect repellent, and now I was concerned but I was not as worried as I had been about my own safety. Although it was really bloody freezing that night, by comparison I slept in relative luxury. I only awoke a few times, gasping for air.

Wednesday 9th September

I got up relatively late; I had eventually slept quite well. We had breakfast at about 9.00 a.m. after the normal routine of my Englishman's wash in what was very fresh sunshine. Today was the day of lunch with Rebecca at Puka Wasi over yonder; so we left at around 10.30 a.m. and walked up the street to the edge of town up onto an Inca pathway that must have been at least five hundred years old. There was a beautiful serenity about the hike up the mountain path towards Puka Wasi, a village of less than one hundred people, a village that stood upon a majestic slope that looked down upon Apuquri itself. We walked up the dirt path, aligned with hedges and old grey stone walls. We hiked for more than an hour, through the cákras all around us, across streams and past some empty rectangular concrete pools that had been built years before, to farm trout, they were then entirely redundant. We passed the occasional campesino walking down with a dog or riding on horseback along the way. We were always, of course, greeted with great warmth and sincere courtesy.

As we reached the last few metres of our ascent, at first sight of the village, we saw a long procession of school children dressed in brightly coloured orange and red-patterned clothes. They were walking along a path on the top of the steep grassy green slope above us. All the children stood in line and waved at us laughing and smiling, and we waved back, it was an uplifting sight. We continued up the path across the one dirt road that came up along a cliff side into a sun drenched Puka Wasi with a fabulous view of Apuquri below.

The village itself was absolutely beautiful, it had an atmosphere of peace and tranquillity that is hard to describe. There was the rare sight of a few tall trees clustered nearby the adobe houses which were all well-kept. The earthen pathways through the village were bordered with grass that had the appearance of a well-tended lawn and I was impressed that there was no litter in sight, despite the lack of any normal public sanitation service.

Marie Paz and I walked through the centre of the village past the fine grey concrete town hall, which had a concrete basketball court below opposite, where there were a group of young boys playing. We turned up yet another steep slope to walk to the top of the village where there was a small group of adobe houses with narrow paths between them that sat at the edge of the village. Puka Wasi was far higher than Apuquri, which looked tiny resting on the mountainside at 500 or 600 metres beneath us; Puka Wasi had a tremendous vantage point overlooking the valleys below, it was still more isolated than Apuquri and felt incredibly peaceful and undisturbed.

We walked up a narrow alley between some ancient unpainted adobe houses, when we stopped at a kitchen door where there were various animal parts hanging up to dry on a cord along the front of the terraced houses, just beneath the roof tiles. Rebecca was cooking lunch in a kitchen much like Marie Paz's, except the food was cooked over a wood fire. Marie Paz normally only cooked in that way when the gas had run out, she had the use of a twin gas burning hob, which was a luxury item. Otherwise the kitchen was very similar in style, it was dark, the floor was earthen, it was dusty, the ceiling around the chimney hole above the wood fire was blackened from the smoke. It was a minimalist kitchen that put the meaning of rustic on another level. It was also much larger than Marie Paz's, it possessed an old wooden table with wooden benches along two sides, where we were to sit and eat.

Rebecca was incredibly hospitable; she was a small dark haired woman in her early forties, who didn't wear quite so many skirts as was the tradition. She was a powerful personality who normally lived and worked as a school teacher in Chalhuanca below. As we walked into the kitchen, Marie Paz immediately sat down at the table to help prepare some of the food. It was an honour to be invited to lunch; for which we had a soup made of lamb stock, with potatoes and various herbs followed by lamb's liver and rice. The meat was incredibly tender and succulent, entirely unlike a lamb's liver bought at Sainsbury's (there are other supermarkets of course). The reason being that Rebecca had killed the animal that morning, two hours before we had arrived; that must put any 1st World organic farmers markets to shame.

After a short while, the old lady from next door came round to join us, she wore many large, traditional, flowing, layered skirts. However on this occasion, not as are often brightly coloured, and she wore the obligatory tall fedora type of hat which is the style of many Peruvian, and also Bolivian women.

There is some debate but some say that at the turn of the 20th century silver mining was prevalent on the Altiplano of Bolivia, where they built railways to transport the ore for processing and export by train to Argentina. It is said that at the time a railway company in Bolivia ordered a large batch of fedora hats for the railway workers. When the hats arrived they were too small for the workmen, so they gave them to the local women who lived on the Altiplano in Bolivia. The hats became very popular and in this way a fashion was born. To this day women can be seen throughout Bolivia and Peru wearing a tall old fashioned style of Fedora, normally worn tilted to one side.

The old lady had a pleasant manner, she didn't have too many teeth, but those that she did have were on display in various directions most of the time. I think she must have had the same dentist as Hercules. I would imagine she was over 90 years old and quite sprightly for her age or even for someone a lot younger. She was quite quiet and sat to one side whilst we ate, she also shooed the young lamb away that had walked in to the kitchen to join us for lunch. The old lady had a very peaceful, tranquil quality about her.

The main topic of conversation was the problem of the miners, I felt quite safe up there discussing the matter in Puka Wasi. I knew that Rebecca, as a well-respected teacher, was not a friend of the miners and had some influence in the community. We were eating in her parents' house, she was only visiting, because her real home was down in Chalhuanca. This meant that she was considerably more worldly than most of the community.

When we had eaten Rebecca showed me the store next door, where the herbs and some of the meat were hung to dry. The herbs were crushed, fresh or dry, in the traditional way in an ancient grey stone shaped as a shallow bowl,[xxxvi] using another long narrow tubular curved stone to mash them, as had been done for hundreds of years. I looked at one of the shelves on the walls above us, and there was the head of the sheep that had been killed that morning, its eyes were smiling at me, from beneath a fine pair of horns.

Rebecca then took me and Marie Paz for a walk in the field adjacent, on a slope that rose at the back of the houses. It was quite large, at least three hectares in size. Rebecca showed us the various herbs that were growing tall in abundance. She told me in what way each type of herb was beneficial for maintaining good health. It seemed that thyme and oregano are used quite a lot in tea and cooking for digestive purposes. Rebecca showed me so many other herbs that were used for so many other ways of maintaining good health that I couldn't remember them all. Without any request, Rebecca cut us huge bunches of the most marvellous fresh herbs. She took a bunch and said, inter alia, this is good for the digestion, this is good for your thoughts, this is good for your kidneys, this is good for your heart, this is good for your liver, this is good for your circulation and so we filled a couple of plastic bags, the herbs were to last us for quite some time.

We said our farewells before Marie Paz and I walked back down through the village to the ancient Inca trail en camino to Apuquri. I said hello, well in fact "hola" and talked to a couple of small black pigs that we met on the way; and so they accompanied us along the pathway for a while, which was highly amusing. A small caravan of horses being brought up the hill passed us on the way down; we were of course greeted with the usual respectful pleasantries.

When we finally got back down to Apuquri, at around 4.00 p.m., we went directly to the building works. It was important that we were seen, almost as dignitaries, to make sure that the workers were able to voice any concerns that they may have had about the project and any materials or tools that they may have needed, not least because we hadn't seen Juan Carlos since Sunday. We were told that he had arrived on a lorry earlier from Chalhuanca with some timber which would be used as lintels for the doors and windows; as soon as it was unloaded, he had gone back to Chalhuanca on the same lorry. The lads were drinking and were in a good mood. They offered us some of the local beer with coke, which didn't taste quite as bad as it sounds.

We drank it in the usual way, from one small plastic cup that was passed around with the obligatory salute to Pachamama and Pachamama.

All was well on the site, so we walked up the incredibly steep slope back to Marie Paz's house. My lungs were fortunately beginning to feel better, but I still had to stop sometimes as I was breathless quite often. We met Victor who was drinking with a couple of other men on the way; they had been working in the cákras that day. They offered us some more shots of cañazo, which of course I had to accept, it would have been rude not to, and I wasn't complaining. If memory serves, Marie Paz also had a couple of shots of that incredibly strong rum, which she didn't drink often. Victor was a great bloke; I admired him as one of the few who, as Rebecca, had also stood up against the miners. I discovered that he had worked in mines elsewhere, which meant he had some money, but he was opposed to the miners taking over Apuquri; and this was incredibly refreshing to know. I was extremely impressed by the generosity of these people, in spirit both in rum and in the essence of their character.

Marie Paz and I continued back up the slope, when we got home she cooked another fabulous meal in her rustic kitchen. A few of those organic celebrity chefs could learn a lot from these people. We talked a while and went our separate ways to bed. The cold was harsh as always, but once I was in bed under eleven blankets, it wasn't so bad.

I woke up at about 3.00 a.m., surrounded by impenetrable darkness all around me, the smallest sound echoed in the night. I turned from side to side as I mulled over whether the miners were concerned about my presence, and I knew they could be ruthless. Perhaps it was the freezing cold at altitude, or the choking for lack of oxygen. I'm not sure, but I didn't get back to sleep until around 5.00 a.m.

Thursday 10th September

I woke up to a beautiful, crisp, clear, sunny day at around 8.00 a.m. and took my usual Englishman's wash of the morning, while Marie Paz cooked us breakfast. Whilst we ate I spoke again to Marie Paz about the danger of confronting the miners. She told me that although the teacher was murdered nearby, which was not the most pleasing thing to hear, she reassured me that that wouldn't happen to me. I don't think that Marie Paz believed that they would do anything against either of us but nonetheless it became quite apparent that she was quite prepared to give up her life for the community if it came to that. She again reassured me that the community would protect me, how, I do not know, but it did make me feel a whole lot better. In retrospect the fear of the unknown is powerful thing, I was, after all, more than a stone's throw away from what to me was the normality of life in so called civilisation, and perhaps I was a little overly concerned.

At about 10.00 a.m. we walked together with Cabo and Saltarin down to work and attempted to buy some nails for the roof on the way into town, but to no avail. This was not a problem but it meant that we would have to go to Chalhuanca at some time soon, where we could generally buy what we needed.

We arrived at the job before 11.00 a.m. to find that there was no one there, which was odd. It came about that it was fiesta time, but no one had told me, which is of course the hazy lazy like, kinda crazy like, South American way.

The way of the custom in Peru seems to be that they don't really tell you everything because the idea is not to create disharmony in anything. It was similar what I have found in North America where you are not really told what the plan is, until you are about to realise it. When Marie Paz noticed that the workers were absent for the day, she was quite happy, she smiled and told me we were invited to a fiesta in the village near our house. That is the part that I do not understand, they all know that there are fiestas and celebrations, but there seemed to be no advance warning, things just happened.

So we walked back up the hill and turned right along our street, to go to a house nearby, not too far along from Marie Paz's place. We walked through a gate into the grey stone walled garden of a typical rustic adobe house, where we were presented with what to me was a very strange scene. I did not feel particularly comfortable.

There were about fifteen people in the garden, some of whom were already quite drunk, well before midday. The people seemed to be of a different type to those I knew already. They were polite as always but they didn't communicate much, they kept their distance and were quite reserved, unlike the builders.

They were all drinking and eating but fairly quiet except for the few musicians in one corner who were playing the occasional traditional harp, violin and intermittent drum. The music had a distinctive sound to it, as though it had been transported in, direct from China. There was a professional dancer, who danced on occasion in a very strange style, which I later learned, is known as "Tijera".[xxxvii] This is a very difficult dance to describe. It embodies a type of gymnastic dance to a strange Chinese drum tempo accompanied by a harp, a high pitched violin and a strange looking instrument that stands like a double bass. Tijera is a fascinating dance form where the performer holds a metal scissor like percussion instrument in one hand, dancing in small jump like movements and flicking and bending his or her feet in a most unorthodox way, at a rhythm seemingly slightly out of time to the music.

The food was very basic, as was the chicha and the rum, which were provided in the customary fashion by a couple of the older ladies present, who were in rotation, in many skirts. Across the lawn, on the other side of the garden, I saw a very pink Cuy,^{xxxviii} having its skin scraped off over a boiling cauldron, this was not the most pleasant sight, I have to say.

We were given a plate of pasta, a glass of chicha and a glass of rum. We didn't stay long, it all seemed a little subdued and a little too much for me, it was time to go because as it turned out, it was a pre-election party. Again no one had told me of what was planned, why I do not know. I was told that we were to go up to Puka Wasi.

A group of us walked out into the street where we all climbed into the back of a waiting open pick-up truck, to drive up to Puka Wasi over yonder. It was a fairly unnerving ride, standing holding on to the roof bars, as the high sided open truck wove along the rough cliff side road, bouncing through the enormous potholes. There were about fifteen of us in the back, where one lady sat, breast feeding her child, and of course that was a perfectly natural thing to do.

We arrived at Puka Wasi after a fifteen minute ride and walked down to what was the main village green where the majority of the whole local congregation were gathered. The green itself was about the size of four tennis courts lined up next to each other, it was a rustic undulating lawn with a large Peruvian flag on a 6ft pole stuck in the middle of it surrounded by many tall trees; this was unusual, trees were not abundant in that part of the world. I had noticed that in Apuquri there were hardly any trees at all. There was a path leading across what seemed to be a relatively well kept lawn that flowed from the road to the green, along which came a procession of people led by the same Tijera dancer and her very small son, who must have been all of seven years old. The dancers were wearing traditional, somehow oriental dress, in a style that you might expect to see in China. The mother had "Vengadora" emblazoned across the front of her purple sash in glittering gold and "Puquio" across the back. She wore a pleated purple skirt as heavily embroidered in golden coloured thread, as was her brightly tasselled purple waist coat. She wore a fedora decorated with a fern leaf poking up from the blue and yellow hat band. They both wore black plimsolls, the son wore white trousers, under black culottes, and a white shirt, over which he also wore a purple waistcoat heavily embroidered in gold, and an embroidered purple skirt that hung over his trousers; he had a very large hat which seemed to be inverted, bigger than his head, which was adorned with thick vertical green and purple stripes, with gold and red tassels hanging all around from the circular red rim at the top.

The lively procession was accompanied by music from a large bass type violin, a normal violin and a slow paced drummer. Most of the people walked out to greet the procession as it moved towards us along the old pathway towards the green. We all then proceeded to return to sit in lines around the edge of the open lawn to watch the dancers. They had been hired for the fiesta from Puquio; they were quite talented in what was probably the strangest form of dancing that I have ever seen, accompanied by traditional music that again, was not entirely dissimilar to that which one might expect to hear in China. There seemed to be some connection with the Orient which was quite surprising. I noticed that the majority of the villagers had narrow eyes and were Mongolian in appearance; though not pronounced, the likeness was all too apparent.

As we sat around the edge of the green in this beautiful place, where the taste of the air was crisp and clean, where we looked down upon the Andean valleys below, the more senior ladies of the village offered us chicha and rum shots, which of course I had to accept, and again I was not complaining. The men all carried shovels or picks as a mark of their solidarity, to show that they working for the community. Most people were in a buoyant mood apart from one man who was lying face down on the opposite side of the green. He was clearly absolutely plastered, but, as I was reliably informed, he had been organising the whole event and had been up from early that morning, and so being drunk, was quite acceptable, it brought no shame on him at all. In fact the day at work in the cákras was known to be accompanied by plenty of chicha and rum shots, which were good for the soul apparently.

When the first round of Tijera was over, it was time for announcements and the proposals for the elections of the dignitaries. This was all performed with a great deal of formality, and what was said was concise and to the point. That said, most of the candidates were fairly drunk by this time, though nonetheless the elections went very smoothly and all was put in order by a show hands. I believe that El Presidente was re-elected, from beneath his drunken fedora.

Once the election process was completed and El Presidente had been voted in for his second and final year or term.[xxxix] The water availability was discussed along with the manner of the cultivation of the cákras. These matters were extremely important, if the water supply was not used correctly or the cákras were not sewn at the right time in the right way, the community would starve and, though unlikely, some of the people could die. It's very easy to disconnect with the reality of the significance of agriculture, especially if the closest most of us in Europe get to a farm is Tesco. There are other supermarkets.

These people lived with the natural world and were incredibly healthy. The modern institutionalised environment disconnects us from nature to such a degree that we now seem to think that antibacterial wipes are important and mud and dirt is a bad thing. This is utterly ludicrous, we are designed to live with bacteria, and without it we could not survive. We are designed to live alongside the earth and nature; we are not supposed to be closeted away in a sanitised antibacterial state. I have seen the dermatitis caused by the constant use of antibacterial hand wipes, as enforced by Health and Safety. As I have said I believe that those responsible should be held at Her Majesty's pleasure, with no remission.

By way of explanation, if you take a lab-rat that has been born from several generations that have never been outside the clinical surroundings of the laboratory, and you breathe on it, that may be enough to finish it off. However if you take a rat that lives in the filth and detritus of the sewers, nothing will touch it. Sewer rats are immune to practically everything, and consequently incredibly strong and healthy.

Naturally, the same applies to our sanitized comfort zone, within which we all live, in the Western World.

* * *

When the elections and the orders of the meeting were over, it was time for a great big party and everyone had no difficulty in deciding to carry on drinking. The Tijera dancer gave another fabulous display with her cocky little son and all was well with the world. Some people got up to dance on the green. I was introduced to several members of the community who treated me with a great deal of respect; I took great pleasure in this customary politeness. The whole experience was entirely uplifting; I even had a dance with Rebecca.

As the Fiesta on the Green, or the Party in the Park, subsided, several people, including myself, began to walk up the steep slope to Rebecca's house, where they sat lining the alley walls outside. As dusk began to fall upon us, we were each given a wholesome bowl of chicken soup that had been prepared by the ladies of the community. I took it upon myself serve shots of cañazo[xl] to the assembled party as we listened to a local radio station and the dogs had at least three vicious skirmishes in front of us. These fights were quickly broken up by a good beating with large sticks and few harsh words. I hasten to add that no animals were harmed or injured in any way during the operation of this fiesta.

When the eating and drinking was done, and as the darkness, and the chill of the evening came upon us, it was time for a group of us to return to Apuquri. We walked back down the steep stony track to the grass road below and jumped into the back of the same, now illuminated, pick-up truck that was waiting to take us back down to Apuquri. I stood up and held onto the bars that curved above the back of the wagon as we drove along down the rut filled, cliff side road, which had been cut into the mountainside, the fresh crisp air filled my lungs. The lights below were incredibly inviting and it must be said that it was quite an exhilarating ride beneath the stars, bouncing along that road, not least due to the uplifting effect of the mixture of cañazo and chicha. We were all very happy; we were all quite drunk, including the driver no doubt.

It was only 8.00 p.m. when we were dropped off outside a local store, not far from Marie Paz's place. So of course we decided to share a few beers outside the store. I was passed a few glasses so in return I made sure that I returned the favour. We stood in the street, in the dark of night, laughing and joking, and making fun of each other. I was something of a novelty and was introduced to some more of the locals, one of whom was called Gringo, clearly because he was a blue eyed teenager; we all had a very good time, rest not with the merchant, dwell with the artisan.

I was in bed by 9.30 p.m. and slept right through until 8.00 a.m. despite the cold, and the choking lack of oxygen.

Friday 11th September

Following my usual Englishman's wash, Marie Paz cooked me another delicious breakfast and we walked down to work for the morning at around 9.00 a.m., with the dogs of course. When we arrived there was no one there, we thought we were about to lose another day, but fortunately, shortly afterwards, Roger, Hercules, Constantino, Don Fernando, and Peso arrived. I was pleased to see them. I didn't want to miss another day. We all worked until about 12.30 p.m. when Marie Paz arrived to take me to a sort of post-election garden party that I had been invited to by one of her neighbours. Again it wasn't too far from our house; this time it was just across the way, a little further along the road, slightly lower down the slope of the hill.

We stepped down from the street into a stone walled garden where we were greeted with a warm welcome accompanied by an obligatory glass of chicha, provided of course by one of the elder ladies in many skirts. In one corner of the garden was a man playing a traditional violin, one playing a trumpet and another playing percussion. There were a couple of people dancing and occasionally the Tijera dancer, from the day before, might give a small demonstration, the difference being that she was slightly drunk as were almost everyone at the party. On another side of the garden there were a few women preparing some soup and some meat, rice and potatoes for our delectation.

The people there were extremely polite as always. I was cordially introduced to a few of them and then me and Marie

Paz were offered a seat. We were then provided with a plate of rice and potatoes in a herbal broth with a little meat. We were also offered the occasional bottle of beer, with a small glass to drink and pass on in the usual way. The musicians were playing and the dancer was dancing, most of the people were drunk but somehow the atmosphere of the place again seemed strangely subdued. It didn't help my sensibilities when I looked up whilst negotiating my potato broth to see a woman, on the other side of the garden, again scraping the last of the fur off another dead, seemingly naked Cuy, whilst it dangled over a boiling cauldron. I began to feel quite uncomfortable.

Marie Paz was quite sensitive to my feelings, she noticed that I wasn't at ease almost immediately; she suggested that we leave when we had finished our food. It wasn't so much the naked Cuy, it was the nature of the drunken people, as they fell about the place, at such an early hour of the day. I make no judgement about that, as before, it is quite acceptable, in that part of the Andes; it is just that I wasn't used to being quite so far outside my comfort zone. We sat quietly for a short while and made our polite excuses and left. That party really did not suit me at all.

When we got back to the house Marie Paz cooked some herbal soup which I was very pleased to consume, and then I must have had a nap. Sometimes the thin air had greater effect than at others, it seemed to catch up on me. When I arrived back at the job at around 3.00 p.m. the others were already working, so I just mucked in, carrying bricks, well actually one adobe brick at a time, of about 70lbs or 35 kilos, on my shoulder. I carried the bricks, up a ladder balanced against a wall at about 45 degrees, then, I would have to balance along the top of what was a 225mm, or nine inch, wall^{xli} and hand the adobe bricks to Roger or Don Fernando who were laying the bricks in muck. Meanwhile Hercules was walking through the muck to collect buckets of muck from Constantino, the old guy with the walking stick, who was standing in the muck, in bare feet with his trousers rolled up, mixing muck for Hercules to carry to Roger and Don Fernando so that they could use the muck to lay the bricks that I carried to build the walls, to build the house so that the kids could go to school.

One adobe brick is coincidently about the same size as, and weighs about the same as, twelve English bricks. This, strangely enough, is the same amount of bricks that fit into a hod that is used to carry bricks on the shoulders of hod carriers, to bricklayers in England. I really enjoy that kind of work, especially in the mountains. It was like being in the gym, but in the fresh air, where everyone was laughing and joking; and we were actually building something worthwhile. We could see what we had achieved at the end of each day and no one could argue otherwise.

The work itself was not entirely dissimilar to that of a building site in England; except of course that we were way up high in the Andes, at around 3,700 meters above sea level, where the air was slightly thinner than I had been used to. The language was Spanish, with a bit of Quechua thrown in, the words were different, but the meaning was in essence the same. The form of the building materials was different, but the basic building format was also in substance the same.

Occasionally in England someone might bring their dog in to work but no one I have ever seen nor heard of has arrived at work with their pet lamb in tow. This particular lamb was called Rosita, and she liked to follow Roger. It was also not overly common in England for a couple of donkeys,

122

or a group of cows for that matter, to wander onto the site whilst we were working; but apart from that, working on a building site in the Andes is not entirely dissimilar to any other on which I have worked.

* * *

I began to realise that I could do the work without getting out of breath too often, or falling off a wall or a ladder for that matter; it was a wonderful, breath-taking job, it had rained a little that afternoon but that didn't matter at all. It was such a beautiful, peaceful, place, I began to feel as though I was on cloud nine, or possibly under it.

We cleared up as usual and put all the tools in the ancient old stone storehouse, close to the site. I then walked up the hill as normal with Hercules. I got home at about 5.45 p.m., we had achieved quite a lot that day.

When I got home, I got changed out of my mucky work clothes and as the night fell upon us Marie Paz and I went for a walk up along the street. We walked with Saltarin our recently acquired dog and Cabo, our resident old faithful friend; we hadn't seen Coaser for a few days.[xlii] As the dogs walked with us, they would systematically bark or growl and see off any other dogs that we met along the way. They stayed with us until they were too far away from their own territory, when they stopped and turned back. Marie Paz and I walked on for about a quarter of a mile, out into the mean streets on the edge of town. There were many dogs that would suddenly bark and growl at us from the darkness, as we passed close by; the walk was actually quite an unnerving experience.

After a few hundred yards, we eventually arrived at the house that we were looking for. Marie Paz's friend was a middle aged woman, of many skirts, who was incredibly pleasant. We were invited into her house which was in fact, quite posh in relative terms. It had a concrete floor, a rare luxury in Apuquri. The walls were also quite upmarket, they had been plastered (by Don Fernando apparently) and the house had been whitewashed inside. The house was however, quite sparse. I remember that there was one picture of the Virgin Mary on a wall, a bare table and a couple of chairs, and possibly a TV, and little else. The house was very small, no woodchip on the wall, there was a living room and a tiny kitchen and there were a couple of bedrooms upstairs. The bathroom was most likely outside at the back which was customary in Apuquri in consequence of the lack of a modern sewerage system. We were promptly provided with a bowl of maize soup which was absolutely delicious. The reason why we were there, I think, was to try and find a taxi for the next day, for which we had no luck. It was quite a formal meeting. The conversation was very polite and genteel, such as you might expect the cucumber triangles to be brought out in anticipation of the arrival of the local Vicar.

When we had eaten, we said our farewells and stepped out into the darkness on the edge of town once more, to face the onslaught of the intimidating ravenous hounds. The walk back was again quite unsettling in fact, but I didn't let that show and our promenade proved to be uneventful, thankfully.

* * *

Whilst we sat at the dining table watching TV with Saltarin later that evening, I complained of a minor strain, I had pulled a ligament or something similar. Upon examination Marie Paz told me my forearm was slightly inflamed and so she disappeared into a back room, from where she produced her very own homemade dark green potion in a plastic bottle. It was a concoction of local herbs that Marie Paz had mixed with a type of alcohol solution. The main ingredient, I was reliably informed, was a herb that could only be found on the slopes surrounding Apuquri, the name of which I will not divulge. Marie Paz rubbed her hands together and warmed them on the flame of a candle, she then massaged my arm with the herbal alcohol; she then held her hands, about an inch above my arm, palms down, as though she were performing some kind of Andean Reiki. After a few minutes treatment she said, "There that should be enough, that should reduce the inflammation and your arm should feel a lot better in the morning."[xliii] She was right, it did.

We stayed up for a little while talking about the imperfections of the charity, which at first did seem quite dreadful, after all, a certain gentleman, who was paid a salary, did have an uncanny habit of disappearing for several days at a time. Nonetheless at the end of the day, no commercial firm is entirely perfect and it would be extremely unreasonable to unfairly criticise a project that was providing funds to build the Casa Hogar, so that the children of the community could gain an education.

I went to my room and got undressed in the bitter cold; I had taken up the practice of balancing on my shoes to avoid getting the grit off the floor stuck to my bare feet, and then into the bed. I switched off the light and climbed under the blankets at around 11.00 p.m. I lay under my eleven frazados and looked into the inky black of night; I could hear no cars or trains, no distant murmur of a motorway. There was no wind that night, only the sound of a dog barking sometimes in the distance. I drifted off to sleep.

Saturday 12th September

I got up at round 8.00 a.m., It was a beautiful sunny morning, my arm was feeling entirely healed, the ache and the inflammation had entirely disappeared. I had my obligatory Englishman's wash and partook of our usual breakfast.

Marie Paz walked with me and the dogs to work, just to talk to the lads to check everything was going according to plan. When we got to the site at around 9.00 a.m., Don Fernando, Roger, Constantino, Hercules and Peso were already there preparing the walls to put the wooden lintels across the top of the gaps left in the walls for the windows and doors. In the UK we put the window and door frames in place and build the walls around them. Up there in Apuquri, where we were building with adobe bricks, not rock solid uniform kiln-fired English bricks, they do it the other way round. They fix the window and door frames to the space in the wall; this does seem a far more cumbersome methodology, but that is the way it is done.

I marked a red line with a chalked cord, with Hercules, level around the inside wall of the room we were working in. Using that line as a marker I began measuring the heights and levels of the lintels as they were put in place on a thin bed of adobe mud. By some kind of natural process I found myself directing the gang. Surprisingly enough, we actually became quite efficient; we managed to put several lintels in situ that morning without too much difficulty at all.

When we were fitting the lintels I taught the lads a little English, which I translated for them. I taught them that when something is good, it is described in English as "the dog's bollocks" (or "the dogs") and if something was bad it was referred to as "bollocks", or a "load of bollocks"; which could of course relate to something in the plural or indeed the singular. I was pleased to notice that they thought that the learning of such an English expression was the dogs. So hopefully, to this day, there is still a group of workers in Peru describing their work in a way that only English, and now Peruvian, workmen know how.

* * *

In that part of the world, there lives a species of large grey bee that appears to have long arched black lines on its face that resemble massive eyebrows, that appear to stem from two tiny black eyes. It has no name in Spanish but is called a Hururunjay[xliv] in Quechua. This type of bee doesn't hive like ordinary bees. It leads a relatively solitary life and lays its egg in a piece of honey, the size of a generous lozenge, normally in a burrow it makes in the side of a tree. Most of the children know where to look for these natural "sweets" but sadly I never did find one. The bee also has another aspect to it; it has the habit of landing on you, with those enormous eyebrows staring, looking straight into your eyes, then out comes a long black sting from its mouth, and if it succeeds in biting you will suffer a severe fever for a few days, unless, as I was told, you have been stung before and have developed a resistance to it.

When we were having a morning chicha break, Roger, who was as always his normal jovial self, caught one of these bees by the wings between two fingers. He smiled at me and showed me the bee and said, "Watch this." The bee was looking at me, from beneath those massive eyebrows, as Roger held its wings gently between his fingers. Roger then took a thin piece of straw,[xlv] about 8 inches long, from the ground. I am sure that when Roger stuck the straw up its back side, it was quite surprised to say the least, as I think anyone would be. It raised its eyebrows by about a foot and a half, and its eyes bulged to twice their normal size. I can only describe its expression as likened to that of a certain Tory Prime Minister, only he has proportionately slightly smaller eyebrows. Then with a huge smile on his face Roger let the bee go and it flew off with that long piece of straw still hanging out of its rear end. That was a very, very odd sight. At first it was very funny, which it was, because it was so unusual to see such a thing; but then it was quite hard on the unfortunate bee, and not something that I would recommend or condone.

* * *

It was a normal day at work except that I appeared to have again been put in charge of putting the lintels in; a job which we managed to complete that day. Marie Paz came down at around 5.00 p.m. and we talked about how we were going to put the roof on. It turned out that the roof was to be made of "Calamina" or corrugated iron. In my mind this plan needed to be changed to Teja Andina[xlvi] or Spanish style clay tiles. The corrugated iron would not act as a heat insulator, it would need to be changed in around ten years and it would be incredibly noisy when it rained. Whereby the Teja Andina had some insulation properties, it would not be nearly so noisy in the rain, and should last for up to 100 years, with some relatively minor maintenance and repairs.

We hadn't seen Juan Carlos since Sunday and were wondering how we were going to change the plan, and also how we would get the money to do so. We decided that I would email the charity in England the following day to see what could be done. It would be a real shame if we had to put a tin roof on the Casa Hogar.

As we walked back home, Marie Paz and I met the Mayor of the town, El Presidente, as he was taking a stroll with one of his assistants. He was a really amenable guy, as usual he was wearing his customary Fedora and a big smile, which may have been something to do with the fact that he was also customarily mildly drunk as was his assistant; they had red rings around their eyes and that slightly vacant expression of people who have had a few. They were more than happy to share a bottle of beer, or two, with us in the street, just in front of Marie Paz's house. I didn't quite understand all that was said when we exchanged pleasantries over those couple of beers. The Alcalde spoke very quickly and wasn't altogether too fond of the use consonants that day. We spoke in that type of language which is entirely courteous but doesn't actually say very much, it is a use of words, so gracious that it creates a social separation; and then we went our separate ways.

We had a normal evening; Marie Paz treated my arm again with the wonder herb, while we watched one of the two available TV channels, though we did channel hop occasionally, just to see what was on. That secret herb was a phenomenal cure; it seemed to repair my arm very quickly indeed. We discussed farming it and selling it to alleviate the financial problems of the community, and the inflammatory problems of the world. But this was an entirely alien process and somehow it seemed that the town didn't want that kind of change.

A crop produced for the basis of financial gain would ruin the way of life, and that was not something that would help the community at all. The irony was that the community did need more money than it had, at times when the harvest may not have been so good. Nonetheless, if they did become significantly more wealthy it was clear how potentially harmful that could be. It seems that without suffering of some kind we never really appreciate what we have; it was as though the austere, sparse periods in life were as necessary as the plentiful times. In the modern world this is often forgotten, but it can be seen quite clearly in religious doctrine throughout history, something is to be understood from that. Muslims do, after all, have Ramadan and Christians have Lent, both of which appear to stand to reason.

I drifted off to sleep that night at around the usual time under my eleven blankets. I wasn't gasping for breath, and I wasn't freezing, I wasn't even getting bitten to death, I might just have been getting used to life in the mountains. Through the silence, as I fell asleep, I could hear the occasional dog barking in the distance, but that was all.

Sunday 13th September

I got up at 9.30 a.m., it was a Sunday, so I didn't have to work, not that the day of the week really made any difference. That morning the sun shone so brightly, that it was quite hot in the garden when we ate our fried eggs for breakfast. Marie Paz and I then proceeded, well mainly Marie Paz proceeded, to wash all of my dirty clothes in the garden, using a couple of buckets, a hand brush and a standpipe.

Cleo Fé was chasing her cows and chickens as usual; she was actually quite fit, she was very sprightly for a woman in her eighties, and she needed to be to chase the cows. She called me over and showed me a wound between the shoulders of one of her cows. It had been bitten by a vampire bat during the night. The wound takes longer to heal than normal because the bat has an anticoagulant in its saliva, for ease of flow when drinking. It was interesting to see the wound of a real vampire bat, and it hadn't really harmed the cow at all. I noticed that the sunshine didn't seem to have a negative effect on the cow either; clearly we did not have to concern ourselves over "The attack of the Vampire Cows".

Shortly afterwards Cleo Fé disappeared into her kitchen and returned a few minutes later to treat us with a bowl of herbal broth, garnished with potatoes and a little meat. It seemed that the people of Apuquri took a great deal of pride in the sharing of food, an expression of love that they are taught from a very early age. There were no tramps in the streets, and there was no apparent crime. Marie Paz told me that if anyone was hungry the community would always look after them. There had been times however when the village was really poor, when the crops had not been as good as they might have been in the past the people couldn't feed so many dogs, so the numbers dwindled in the streets.

We went into town to meet a carpenter apparently, to organise the construction of the windows and door frames to fit in the Casa Hogar, which again was something that Juan Carlos should have been arranging. Through the grapevine it appeared that Juan Carlos had reappeared once more, but we hadn't seen him. When we got downtown we couldn't find the carpenter, but fortunately we did find a taxi to take us to Chalhuanca, for Sol. 5 each; a taxi which of course we shared with half the people of the village.

When we got down to Chalhuanca mid-morning, we bought the nails that Don Fernando had asked us for the previous day, again something which Juan Carlos should have been doing. We also did some food shopping, we bought some local cheese in the street and we bought some vegetables; a bottle of rum for me and a few other bits and pieces. We also bought some lamb, which are apparently simply called Carneros in Peru instead of the more common Spanish Cordero or Oveja. Carnero (normally meaning Ram in Castilian Spanish) comes from "Carne" the word for meat, which could be literally translated as "Thing of meat". It was a bit like calling pigs "Porks",[xlvii] or cows "Beefs".[xlviii] Spanish does not have quite the same dichotomy probably because it was not invaded by the French in 1066 a.d. The Moorish invasion of Spain in 711 a.d. did not have quite the same influence on the language.

When we had done the shopping we went to a juice bar in the market building and I bought a couple of fruit juice mixes of mango that were as good as you can get anywhere in the world. We then went for some lunch in one of the local restaurants, where we had the set menu or "menu del día", which was soup, followed by a mixed grill with chips and a sweet of flan, a type of egg custard. The food may not have been Michelin Star standard but it was very good indeed; on par if not better than any European equivalent and it was incredibly cheap.

After lunch I went to the internet café to send a message to the charity about the roof. My girlfriend still didn't seem to like to write, and I hadn't heard from her, which made me sad and disappointed. I wrote to the charity to ask if we could have about £300.00 to build a tiled roof, and I explained why. I also said, "I find myself at the head of the construction project", which may have been a mistake, as I was rebuked for that later. In effect I had taken this role, because Juan Carlos was never there and again he should have been dealing with this. I wasn't very happy with Juan Carlos to say the least, but I couldn't say that he had quite simply disappeared, and that Marie Paz and I were doing virtually all of his work. It was unjust that Juan Carlos was being paid for a job that Marie Paz was doing, and I found that it churned my stomach. It was also disturbing to know that Juan Carlos had befriended the miners and was reported to have been working against the people he was supposed to be supporting. But what could I say? Precisely nothing is all I could say about that. I learned that the situation was so politically sensitive, that no one within the charity was allowed to criticize the senior staff, who in fact numbered two in total, even if they were acting to the detriment of the organisation.

Marie Paz came to collect me from the café at around 4.00 p.m. and we went back to the high street to book my bus ticket back to Lima. I was introduced to a friend of Marie Paz's who was sitting with a bucket of trout, under a covered way along the front of the shops. He told me he normally caught about ten trout a day, during about one hour's fishing in the Apurimac River just behind the main street, where he was sitting. I have eaten those wild trout, they are absolutely delicious, and they are abundant in that particular river. I think the fisherman may have been called Andino Hechero Lugar de Castigo, who may have had a distant cousin called Hugh.

We were informed that a seat for me on an overnight bus to Lima on 27th September at 7.00 p.m. could be bought for Sol. 80 (£16.00) which was not the cheapest, but Marie Paz knew the agent and told me that the bus would be reliable and comfortable. Often what was advertised as a bus having a full reclining seat, almost akin to a bed, bore little relation to what was actually on offer. It was important that the service was comfortable and reliable because the return journey back across the Andes, via Nazca, up the coast back into Lima, takes at least fourteen hours and the road could be extremely treacherous. I never did become accustomed to looking down the side of a cliff from the side of a bus, or indeed from a taxi for that matter, not least, on the way to or from Apuquri.

With the knowledge of the availability and price of a return ticket, we went to the rendezvous point across the road, which we had prepared earlier, for the return taxi journey. The driver clearly had other plans because he simply didn't turn up; so we had to book another, which resulted in me having to pay a vastly inflated price of Sol. 10

(£2) each. It did seem that the price to go up the mountain track to Apuquri was normally a lot more in relative terms; nonetheless I did have the impression that this was probably gringo price, even though I'm not North American. When we arrived at the petrol station in the darkness on the edge of town, it came as no surprise that we were asked to pay in advance. The driver didn't have sufficient money to buy the fuel for the trip otherwise, but that was not entirely uncommon.

After the driver had stopped to buy petrol, he then stopped on the way to collect his wife, which was quite amusing. They'd probably decided to double the trip to take the opportunity to visit some friends in Apuquri. It had become quite dark and there was a chill in the air by the time we turned off the beaten track to get up the rocky mountain road to Apuquri, as we listened to the obligatory Peruvian music, crackling on the radio. I noticed that the driver was driving as though he was thinking of entering a rally competition. Perhaps he thought he was the next Sébastien Loeb or Miko Hirvonen for that matter. The trouble was that as the journey progressed so did his speed, and as we got faster on the rough dirt and gravel road, we seemed to get closer to the cliff edge, as we drove along the ledge that was the road cut into the mountainside. I normally live in the South of England, where there are some hills, but these hills pale into insignificance in comparison to the Andes which are second only to the Himalayas in height. As we drove everyone seemed quite happy, maybe they were glad that the driver had the chance to practice, but I wasn't too comfortable at all and I also didn't want to lose face, which is what would happen if I were to mention that we might be going just a little too fast. I lasted about half an hour when we went so close to the edge of a cliff that I could wait no more. I decided to throw any thought of machismo that I may have had out the window, to me it was getting too dangerous. Then I chickened out and kept my mouth shut, I didn't say a word, I couldn't, the others in the car seemed totally oblivious to any danger whatsoever and I just couldn't show myself up. I watched in silent trepidation until we had driven for what seemed like hours up that track into the hidden conurbation that is Apuquri.

Monday 14th September

I will freely admit that, much to my own embarrassment I woke up late this morning. Juan Carlos arrived to join us for a late breakfast. He had been missing for several days and although we were both appalled by Juan Carlos's absence, we didn't say anything to him about that, not least because he seemed totally oblivious to any misgiving for his part. He was, as always, his normal cock sure jovial self. It may have been that he was just thick skinned; or it may have been that in view of his position, he thought that he was able to do as he wished without fear of retribution.

We walked down to work late at 10.30 a.m., which wasn't a problem at all because the three of us were both regarded as management. We had a meeting with the men at around 11.00 a.m. about the project and in actual fact Juan Carlos was incredibly helpful when he heard about the idea to change the roof from corrugated iron to proper clay tiles. He said that we could change the specification from other parts of the building, such as to put in a concrete floor in place of a wooden floor and use the saving to pay for the roof tiles.

We arranged to change the roof for the sum of Sol. 2500 – 2800, quite a lot of money in Peruvian terms, being around £600.00. The flow of caña[xlix] (another local rum) mixed with yellow Inca Cola smoothed matters over quite considerably, along with a few glasses of chicha, so early in the morning. The chicha was a strange brew, as I have said before it had an incredible effect; it gave such clarity of thought. The old guy, Constantino, passed me the glass for the chicha, and whilst I filled it he looked at me and with a broad smile on his face, he put his left hand on his right bicep, clenched his right fist and bent his right arm upwards. He said in a deep imposing voice, "Es bueno para la prostata" and he was right. He said it would be useful if I wanted to sire one of the local girls; to which all my work colleagues were in agreement, they all thought that that would be a jolly good idea.

The chicha really did appear to clear the system and could cause an embarrassing amount of movement in the trouser department, when least expected. I am not a homosexual and if I was I doubt very much that Constantino would have been my type, so it must have been the chicha. In truth this drink could be a cure for any prostate gland problem anywhere in the world. It seems that chicha is a health giving aphrodisiac, which actually works. This is not entirely dissimilar to sauerkraut I have learned, there are well over 80 million Germans after all.

* * *

I was extremely pleased that we had agreed to change the roof; in my eyes it would have been a calamity to have covered the roof with Calamina.[1] What I wasn't expecting was receiving an incredible amount of respect for this change in the project, because I thought that I had done nothing at all, I'd only provided the idea. Still, as they say, it's the thought that counts.

We didn't do a massive amount of work that morning Juan Carlos and I, we went back to have lunch at 12.30. We had worked for the hour and a half, which was sadly merely a token gesture, in particular on the part of Juan Carlos. It was quite funny to see him wobbling up the occasional ladder on all fours. I guess if you are not used to it there is a lot more to building than meets that eye. For example you shouldn't climb a low slung ladder bent over using your hands, you should just balance upright on the rungs as you walk up it, this leaves both hands free to carry things and shows a bit of bravado. The ladder was well below 45 degrees and to go along it on all fours gave the impression of a novice, or plonker, in the wise words of Peckham.

Another thing you shouldn't do on a building site is stand around doing nothing, gazing at nothing in particular. Back in the day I have seen hod carriers in Hampshire, sent down the road for doing the same. I later learned that before I had arrived, one of the guys, Edwin, had made fun of Juan Carlos a fair amount, for amongst other things, his lack of building skill. The ribbing is part of your apprenticeship as a builder, and Edwin was known as being quick witted. Sadly though, Juan Carlos didn't see it in that way, so he had sacked poor Edwin for having a sense of humour.

Following another delicious herbal enhanced lunch made by Marie Paz we got back to work at around 1.40 p.m. All the lads were already there. Juan Carlos talked to Don Fernando and Roger for a while, said his farewells and disappeared to do some accounts of some sort which I suppose was his prerogative; there was no love lost in his actions, it seemed that it was better that he was gone, the atmosphere on the site became far more comfortable.

The afternoon for me consisted mainly of cleaning the top off the adobe bricks with a Peruvian mattock, in preparation for the next course of adobe bricks. This was very good physical exercise, beneficial for the upper body apparently. The lads made fun of Hercules for a lot of the time, they were saying that he was feeling depressed because he was envious of me living with Marie Paz. They also said that I should be careful, because he had his eye on Marie Paz and I should be wary because of what jealousy might do. This created a strange dichotomy, if you were to consider the normal jokes were about Hercules being gay, nothing wrong with that of course.

While we were working we decided that Hercules should have a pair of golden balls that should be removed and put in a cabinet at home, for safe keeping. We told him that he needed to do some preparation before he could show them to Marie Paz. First of all, he had to become rich, I told him that he needed to go up into the mountains and take some of the gold to make himself wealthy, and then he could have his teeth fixed, have his golden balls made and then, when the girls saw that he had new teeth and some money, they'd all start following him around. The next part of the plan I told him, was that then he should get some practice with some of the other girls before he made a move on Marie Paz; then he could take her home and show her his golden balls, and then, maybe, if he was really lucky, she might marry him.

That is the exactly the same type of rubbish we used to talk on building sites in England. A little crude perhaps, but then again so is a lot of humour. It was all taken in good stead and in fact that type of nonsense lightened the days somewhat. That's the way we amused ourselves, talking absolute bollocks. Sorry about that though Marie Paz, it was only a joke, that said I seem to remember I did tell her something of what was said, which did make her laugh.

We left work at around 5.30 p.m. after we had collected the tools and put them in the ancient stone building adjacent to the works. Hercules and I walked back up the hill together, and as normal he imparted the wisdom of the world upon me, I was grateful for that. He asked me if we had tractors in Europe, to which I told him we did. He shook his head and said, "Not here, everything is natural, we only use bulls to plough the fields, and we don't use any chemicals at all". We all too easily forget that tractors fill the air with smoke and drop oil on the ground, and I imagine even the slow seepage of oil could be cumulative, which could pollute the crop, even if in only a small way.[li]

We met Victor with a couple of his friends once more on the steep incline back to the house. They offered us some rum, which gave a pleasant warmth as usual, in consequence of its strength. Victor had been working high up in the cákras and we enjoyed a few shots in a small field behind a stone wall, by the side of the pathway, on the way.

Marie Paz and I had a normal evening, that evening, but I remember there was the sound of a fiesta that night in the town below, I could hear drums and a traditional Peruvian trumpet in the distance as I drifted off to sleep under my eleven blankets in the freezing cold of the inky black of night.

Tuesday 15ᵗʰ September

I got to work after breakfast at around 9.00 a.m. It was another bright, bright, sunshiny day, working in the light breeze, on the Andean slopes, looking up to the spectacular peaks above us and the distant valleys that spread out below. I was mainly carrying the single 70lb adobe bricks on my shoulder, to Roger and Don Fernando, balancing on the ladder and along the top of the walls, just as if I were a hod carrier back in England except without the scaffolding and without the hod. I absolutely loved doing that work; it was like working out in a gym for free. I was getting super fit at 3,700 meters above sea level. Constantino was mixing the mud and paja as usual, in his bare feet with his trousers rolled up to his knees, with his walking stick resting against a wall nearby; whilst Hercules was carrying buckets of the muck and throwing them up to Don Fernando and Roger. Young Peso was generally helping out, as was normal he generally didn't say very much.

Early that day I was obliged to buy a plastic jerry can of pink chicha for Sol. 5; young Peso was sent to get it from the store. Peso means "weight" in Spanish, which is ironic because we all know the joke about sending the lad to the store for a "long weight" or perhaps some "Tartan Paint". Peso said very little, not surprising really because we were all making fun of whatever we could think of all day; which was generally the same jokes about Hercules' sexuality, he was either gay or jealous of me. Hercules thought it was all very funny, he was generally oblivious to any offence. I guess if Peso had said very much they would have ridiculed him as well, but he kept himself quiet beneath the angst of a young teenager.

We sat on a few adobe bricks for our morning break in the sunshine and drank some of the abundant chicha. It was a fabulous drink, somehow enlightening in actual fact. Of course we drank from one shared plastic cup; this time cut from the bottom an old two litre plastic gaseosa bottle that someone had found lying around the place. I was pleased to be working with a group of artisans building a Casa Hogar in the mountains. These were honourable, honest people who lived with the earth, they were not accustomed to strangers, and I was extremely grateful for their acceptance.

Hercules and I walked up for lunch at the usual time of around 12.30 p.m. I returned with Marie Paz to work after an hour or so and we carried on building. Most of the jokes stopped until Marie Paz had left, she was, as always, treated with an enormous amount of respect, as I believe were all of the women in the mountains, generally speaking of course, after all, this is not a perfect world in which we live.

The afternoon went well; we drank a few more glasses of Chicha as the time passed by. At around 4.30 p.m. we stopped to drink a little of what was a dark rum that they called whisky, which we mixed with coke, which I may well have bought that afternoon as a celebration of something. We found a small plastic glass that we passed around, in the usual way until the bottle was empty. We continued working for a while until 5.30 p.m., and then we cleared up for the day. There is something very satisfying about putting your tools into an ancient stone building when you have done a good day's work.

When the day was almost done, at 5.00 p.m. Juan Carlos had turned up, as had Don Mereno the carpenter. He was probably one of the shortest men I had ever seen, and had the physical aspect of an indigenous man; he had the features of a true Inca. He had come from a nearby village, a couple of hours away, to discuss his potential employment as the carpenter to build the roof timbers. He had no car and had been given a lift to Apuquri by a relative, who was nowhere to be seen. He was a very polite man and was treated with a certain deference in view of his skill as an artisan. He was often referred to as "Maestro", when he was addressed by his fellow workers.

I felt a pang of compassion for Juan Carlos when he turned up at the end of the day, just a pang mind you. He had spent the day detached, moving one piece of paper from one place to another, or in other words sitting on his arse doing very little, but he was all alone. I said to him that I wanted to buy a small bottle of rum for the evening, to drink at Marie Paz's place, which he agreed would be a good idea. I had the taste; after all we had been drinking for most of the day. When we walked up into town to the store, all the lads, including Constantino with his walking stick, followed us up the hill.

Juan Carlos and I walked into the store and the whole team followed us in. I looked around me and bought a large bottle of coke, and a half litre of the local rum. Of course I offered the drink to share and we drank the whole bottle of rum mixed with a little coke, from a single glass in the customary fashion, in a very short time. Everyone was enjoying themselves so I bought another, which we promptly drunk, again from the same single glass. There were no fresh glasses in Apuquri and no one died in consequence.

I was told that the tiny carpenter Don Mereno was not only the last of the Incas, and he certainly looked like he was, he was also a carpenter and a maestro on the violin, which he would play for us on some future occasion; he was justifiably very proud of this. We had a great time standing around in that store drinking, laughing and joking about whatever came upon us; though it was slightly more reserved than usual on account of Juan Carlos's presence. When the rum was finished we all left and walked together to Roger's house, a few blocks up the hill, where we walked into a full house, they were all having a party.

I remember going into the fiesta, I remember being given a bottle of beer and talking to a few people, but, much to my embarrassment, that is pretty much all I remember. I have a vague recollection of swapping baseball caps with Hercules in the bar, walking to Roger's place, talking to a few people and a somewhat blurred memory of being carried down the street, but that is all, I'm afraid, much to my shame.

Wednesday 16th September

I woke up the next morning with blood on my pillow; the veins in my nose had given up to the altitude as had the rest of my being. I felt like someone had been jumping up and down on my head, and I had a pain in one of my thighs, and both of my knees, which were slightly grazed. My right arm wasn't feeling too good either and I appeared to have knocked my bedroom door off its hinges, as it was missing, oh dear.

I felt totally drained, I realised that I must have done something really stupid and made a complete and utter fool of myself, but I couldn't figure out what I had done. I didn't think that I had drunk that much the night before, but I felt dreadful. I didn't even have the energy to get out of bed. Drunkards' remorse had set in big style and the apprehension of what may have happened the night before filled me with dread. I lay there totally incapacitated for at least two hours before I got up and made myself some tea and then went back to bed to sleep for a while; the house was empty, apart from the guinea pigs and the chickens. The dogs had disappeared and Marie Paz was nowhere to be seen.

Marie Paz came back around lunch time; apparently she had been down to the site. I was sitting in the garden reading when she arrived; I was extremely ashamed of having been drunk, and still unsure as to what had happened. I apologised profusely for my behaviour and for the missing door of course. Marie Paz didn't see it that way at all, she had been to see the lads, I mean workers, at the site and she told me that she was extremely annoyed with them. As far as Marie Paz was concerned they were supposed to be looking after me and they had failed to do that. I had come back totally plastered, with a nose bleed and abrasions from a fall, talking absolute nonsense, nothing new there then. In that part of the world drunkenness is not frowned upon in the way it is in Europe, it is considered as a part of life and nothing to be ashamed of. I felt a little better but it did not diminish my chagrin in any way, I still had to face the lads the next day.

Apparently I had been fine until I had got to the party, then I decided that I wanted to look for the last of the Incas, so Hercules, thankfully I might add, had put his arm around my shoulders and walked me home. Unfortunately for me, Hercules was a lot lighter than me, which is why I descended the steps on the way out of Roger's house rather more quickly than I would have liked and had hurt my legs. It was then that I had also decided to become the archetypal drunken idiot who loved everyone in the world by the time we got home. Whilst staggering around the living room I had fallen into the bedroom door and knocked it clean off its hinges and Marie Paz and Hercules had to pick me up again and had put me to bed. I felt like a complete arse, probably because I had landed on my arse.

At first I couldn't understand why I had suffered such inebriation. I hadn't drunk very much more than normal. Then the blatantly bleeding obvious struck me, as had the bedroom door. I hadn't had anything to eat and at more than 10,000 feet above sea level, I was already in danger of suffering from oxygen starvation. With the added bonus of the oxygen depletion in the blood caused by the alcohol, it was like a double whammy and my body had decided, quite rightly so I might add, that it had had enough. The low oxygen levels in the air, combined with the thinning of the blood and the lower pressure at altitude had caused my nose bleed which had added to the devastating effect. I would have to be more careful in the future.

I read a lot that afternoon, and I cleaned the mud off my new Baseball cap, the exchanged gift from Hercules. I was suffering from oxygen starvation and was too weak to go work. Later that afternoon Juan Carlos came by to say hello and to have a cup of tea, which was generally made from fresh muña, which is apparently incredibly beneficial to the digestive system; that or Teronjil which is good for the heart, but sadly no cucumber triangles, or indeed a vicar. Juan Carlos didn't look too good himself in fact, he didn't say too much, he wasn't his usual smiling jovial self either.

Juan Carlos had been down to the job and said something about going to Chalhuanca to get some timber for the new roof. He said that he would have to do the figures to reduce the cost of some of the building, he was sure we could build a proper tiled roof instead of the originally proposed calamine, but he would also have to get some good quotes for the tiles and the roof timbers.

Juan Carlos also said that we may have to make some minor sacrifices, like, for example the wooden floor for the Casa Hogar as he had mentioned or a goat or a small child. In effect the change to the roof looked feasible but the accounts would have to verified, it seemed that Juan Carlos was going to do a good job, but all was not quite what it seemed.

Juan Carlos said he was going to go into town to discover some prices and would email the charity in England to ask for their agreement to the change, which meant that he left quite soon after at 3.00 p.m.

If Juan Carlos could achieve this amendment to the works, that would be really good news.

* * *

When Marie Paz returned early that evening she cooked me some of her health giving herbal infused food, which was probably just what I needed; and I was soon on the road to recovery from that atrocious hangover of all hangovers, and the anguish of my alcoholics' remorse. We stayed up a while and I remember we discussed how in ancient cultures they believed that insecurity and worry would manifest itself in you your life as a very harmful and damaging thing. Which is linked to the belief that we all create our own destiny by the way we think, that moves into faith and persuasion.

It is interesting that the verb to think in Spanish is creer and the verb to create is crear, which is almost the same, both may originate from the same Latin root. It seems then that to think is to create. So I decided that I had better not worry about the miners. I just had to be careful not to talk about the mining rights to the wrong people, which meant anyone except Marie Paz, and Rebecca, and possibly a few other people, most of whom I had yet to meet. It was quite simply too dangerous to do otherwise.

Not really a lot else happened that day. I got into bed by torch light, having turned the main light off. I balanced on my shoes as usual so as not to get the grit from the earthen floor on my feet and into my bed. It was again freezing cold that night and I was very glad of all those blankets.

I was also glad of the insect repellent that I had procured in town; hopefully my hands would not become a meal for hungry Peruvian sand flies.

I drifted off to sleep in the silence of the night broken only by the occasional dog barking in the distance.

Thursday 17th September

It was raining when I woke up that morning, so Marie Paz and I had a leisurely breakfast. There isn't a lot that can be done in the rain on a building site that is open to the elements. So we relaxed and waited until the weather cleared. It was 11.00 a.m. by the time the rain had stopped, the sun began to shine and we got down to the site.

I wasn't exactly looking forward to seeing the men that morning. I knew the jokes would be on me, as the drinks had been that fateful drunken night. The men were incredibly respectful when Marie Paz and I arrived; they were smiling with slight apprehension. They were quieter than usual, almost sheepish in fact. I think they were still nervous from suffering the wrath of Marie Paz the previous day. Personally I thought it was my fault and my responsibility that I had got drunk, but still I was grateful for Marie Paz's concern.

I got to work loading out adobe bricks for Don Fernando and Roger to put in place while Constantino was up to his knees in mud as usual, mixing it up for Hercules to load it out. The hard graft of carrying bricks and mixing muck brings about a peaceful easy feeling. Walking around in mud in bare feet massages all the pressure points in your feet. Peso was bringing dry bricks down to the walls in a wheel barrow, in his usual quiet spoken, slightly surly, teenage sort of way.

Strangely enough, almost as soon as Marie Paz had left, the jokes started. They asked me many times if I had found the last of the Incas and were making fun of me for being drunk, ribbing me all day, but in an amiable way, and I was happy with that.

A whole load of timber, which consisted of rough stripped tree trunks and large bundles of roughly hewed roof battens, had been delivered late by lorry, the previous evening. Don Moreno had begun work with his assistant Oscar, who was a small grey haired man in his sixties, with piercing blue eyes, which were unusual for a Peruvian. They were both very agreeable. The carpenters were slightly less aggressive in their humour than the bricklayers, in a similar way to the trades in the UK where each occupation has a comparable personality. For example scaffolders are generally slightly crazy, as are roof tilers; hod carriers are usually quite young and often enjoy a jolly good fight. Most bricklayers have to carry the hod as part of their apprenticeship before they are allowed to lay bricks, but they are usually incredibly calm men when they get older, which speaks for itself. Plasterers can be quite vibrant and carpenters are generally far more genteel in their ways.

I later learned that in the nineteen eighties Oscar, a very gentle man, had been arrested under suspicion of being a member of the Sendero Luminoso. He had been detained in Abancay by the authorities, which he described to me as something which was a very unpleasant experience. I have the impression that he was kept in jail for a few months and during that time he was interrogated in a most disagreeable manner, but he didn't imply much more than that. I have a sneaking suspicion that he may have been tortured.

Don Fernando and Roger reminded me, with a great deal of amusement that Don Moreno was actually the last of the Incas, and they may have been right, I think I had finally found him. He certainly did have an unusual physical aspect about him. He had a dark complexion, he had dark brown skin was very short, about 5ft tall, but perfectly in proportion, and was incredibly muscular. His face was not European at all, it was slightly elongated, with relatively prominent high cheekbones and his eyes were slightly narrower than those of a Caucasian. He was also more serious than the others; he did make jokes, but not quite so many, and was a very pleasant, courteous man.

We carried those huge bundles of wood down to the site on our shoulders. They were incredibly heavy for me, but for these Peruvian workers, who were seemingly so slight in stature, they didn't appear to be nearly so cumbersome. It took some time for my body to become accustomed to such weight, but for the others this did not seem to be the case at all.

As was normal I walked back up to the house for lunch with Hercules. We parted company at the front of the house and I went in for yet another exceedingly healthy herbaceous meal, already prepared by Marie Paz.

As we were about to have lunch, Cleo Fé turned up with a splinter in her finger. So I took my tweezers from my room and took her hand, as she looked up at me with her innocent eyes, from beneath her fedora. After a couple of minutes of prodding, I managed to pluck the splinter from the old lady's finger. I haven't administered much first aid, and it was very satisfying to see the relief in Cleo Fé's eyes. I was very fond of Cleo Fé and I believe my medical assistance could have meant the beginning of a beautiful friendship. Without wishing to seem melodramatic, it was a wonderful moment.

After lunch, in the clean light sunlit breeze, I helped the carpenters, Don Moreno and Oscar, back at the top of the site, where there was a flat grassy pathway[lii] about 10 metres wide, set atop a slope about 5 metres above the muck and rubble of the general works. To build the roof trusses we had to look for the straightest of the timbers. The most suitable to be trimmed down to be used as braces and cross timbers; our job was to measure them up and cut them to size and the carpentry was quite rustic to say the least. Basically we built triangular roof trusses, in the same geometric shape as that of any European house but out of bare stripped tree trunks and branches, none of which were planed flat, as they would be in Europe. Consequently a lot of the knots had to be removed by Don Valerio. He would rest his boot on the offending knot, and then strike it with a sharpened mattock; it looked as though he was trying to remove the bottom of his foot. Of course we had no electric tools at all, there were only a few hand tools and a chainsaw that was taller than Don Moreno himself, which was used for cutting the timbers. The frames were bashed together with 4 and 6 inch nails, which was not an easy task by any means. The timbers were tough and the nail tips needed to be topped with oil, to bang them in.

At the end of the day, after having built several, large heavy roof trusses, we cleared up and I walked up the slope with Hercules en camino a casa.[liii] We had discussed going to the local Internet Café, so Hercules directed me down a side street to look for the only computer in town which was apparently in someone's front room. The young girl in attendance said that it cost Sol. 2 an hour and it was working, by which she meant that it could be switched on. She wasn't wrong of course, but it wasn't entirely working, it couldn't connect to any internet, anywhere, and I couldn't find out if I had been sent another link. I'm not sure that she was entirely aware of the so called wonder of the internet. So without feeling any disappointment at the fact that there was no internet in all of Apuquri, we walked on up to Marie Paz's place in the grey light of dusk.

We met a few people on the way, who gave us the customary greeting and for some reason I noticed that most of them were covered in a thin layer of grime. In fact most of the people of the village were covered in a thin layer of grime, then I looked down at myself and realised that I was also covered in a thin layer of grime. Did this mean that I had gone native?

We walked up the stone steps and unusually for Hercules, he followed me in. We sat out in the porch, with Cabo and Saltarin lying on the grass beside us, where we drank the beer that I had bought from the store opposite the house. The bright stars shone above, as clear as can only be seen in the Andes, it was a still and quiet evening, apart from the echo of the dogs barking sometimes in the streets and getting into scuffles.

Hercules joined us for supper that evening. He had great admiration for Marie Paz, he was certainly very fond of her. He was a man who appeared to be very innocent, he lived an uncomplicated life. However that didn't stop him talking, about straightforward logical matters, he made a lot of sense, and that night was no exception. Hercules regarded the most important things in life as having enough food to eat and somewhere to sleep, everything else to him was secondary, he would have dearly liked a wife, as would most men, but such is life.

We hadn't seen Juan Carlos for quite some time, however it was interesting to learn that at around 10.00 p.m. the previous evening Juan Carlos had turned up at Hercules' house, and that Hercules had helped unload a lorry load of timber, delivered for the roof. In actual fact Hercules had worked until quite late. When the timber had been unloaded Juan Carlos had then returned to Chalhuanca with the lorry, bless him.

Hercules left the house, quite early in fact, at around 8.00 p.m.; then Olivia, Marie Paz's friend, arrived shortly afterwards wearing the normal, traditional layered skirts and fedora type hat. She was concerned about a transfer of land; for which Marie Paz, being somewhat of an icon, was asked advice. She chatted for a while but she didn't exactly stay very long either, once the anxiety over the land was alleviated. Land was not owned in the normal way of say Europe or the Western World, it was generally owned by the community that worked upon it. In years gone by, the land would become the property of the person who worked it after two years, if the request was made to the authorities the land was granted, but the law had changed. Nowadays if a member of the community wishes to work a particular parcel of land, that person can ask El Presidente for permission to do so and if granted, following a consultation with the community, that land will become the property of said member, and the contract of ownership will be renewed every two years, which will in effect become a rolling two year lease.

Marie Paz's great grandparents have passed several parcels of land down to the family over the years, however to gain ownership of tracts of land of that size within the community of Apuquri was no longer possible. Nonetheless it is possible to own a small holding to farm or upon which to build a house. This is done by a collective group of Apuqurinos who gather together to have a faena,[liv] where they join together to spend a day or so clearing a section of land. They must have three faenas on the same parcel within one year, following those, they may ask El Presidente to divide the land into individual plots, which will then be allocated to become the individual properties of those participants within the faenas.

* * *

When Olivia had gone Marie Paz treated my arm once more with her incredible herbal potion and a little heat from a candle to warm her hands. The National Health Service really would benefit if it could find that anti-inflammatory plant, only known to that specific valley of Apuquri.

That night it was very cold, so I asked Marie Paz for an extra blanket which she very kindly provided before she went to bed, quite early at 9.00 p.m. I now slept under a grand total of twelve blankets. Before bed I warmed myself with a little rum, I needed to, it was so cold that evening I could see my breath whilst was watching TV and reading Stephen Fry's *Moab is my Washpot* at the same time, no mean feat. Coincidently I noticed the man on the TV, who I had seen before, a man quite well dressed, in a jacket and tie, interviewing someone on a high-brow television programme. The interviewer was tall and slim with a foppish fringe, he was so similar to Stephen Fry in appearance, the resemblance was quite uncanny. There, on the TV in front of me, was the Peruvian Stephen Fry, once more. I think he was called Jaime Vaillez, and I would imagine it would be hilarious if they were ever to meet.

After having a shot or so of rum it was easy to fall asleep in the pitch black of the night. I was shielded from the cold under twelve blankets and from the sand flies under yet another layer of insect repellent; having stumbled around, balancing on my shoes trying to avoid getting dry soil on the bottom of my bare feet. I was quite accustomed to the silence of the night, now being occasionally broken, only by the sound of a dog barking somewhere in the distance.

Friday 18ᵗʰ September

Marie Paz and I had a cup of porridge, a herb tortilla and a little toast for breakfast. We sat outside at the table adjacent to the kitchen and looked down the valley from what was the exclusive borough of Apuquri Heights. It was another beautiful sunny day. Apuquri had a quiet tranquillity about it, broken only occasionally by the noise from the sheep, and of course the dogs or someone playing some music in the distance; oh and perhaps the tannoy system announcing the forthcoming elections or the sale of lamb chops or a pork or something else fresh from the Carnicaeria,[lv] when someone had killed some home grown, organic livestock, normally to the tune of one. As would also happen on occasion the tannoy might ask a member of the community to come and collect his or her goat, sheep, cow, bull, horse or Alpaca for that matter, from the bullring where it had been incarcerated for wandering the streets unattended. As it turned out, there was a small fine to pay.

As would happen sometimes, a goat herd or shepherd would pass along the road beneath us with his or her flock, along what seemed to be the entire family. They would always greet us with a wave and a smile, as they wandered past. Cabo and Saltarin usually stood looking down from the top of the wall with their hackles raised, but only slightly. They wanted to show their presence in their territory to the sheep dogs as they walked past. We only saw Alpacas once, at night. Strange as it may seem, I've seen more Alpacas and Llamas in Surrey than I have in Apuquri, which when I come to think of it is quite odd, because they would be useful to the community and are extremely common in Peru. The reason for this lack of these animals is that a few years beforehand three Alpacas were given to the community, un macho, una hembra y un hijo, the male and the kid died of triquina, a parasitic worm. When the mother was killed to eat, the meat was found to be inedible, also infested with triquina. In consequence the community did not wish to keep any Alpacas any more.

* * *

Marie Paz and I went down to work at around 9.00 a.m. accompanied by Cabo and Saltarin. Marie Paz, as usual, had a chat with Don Fernando to make sure that everything was in order, then she went back home with the dogs. My job that day, once more, was to help Oscar and Don Moreno building the roof trusses, but I think, if truth be told, I would have preferred getting covered in mud and massaging my feet.

After lunch we all went back to work as usual, but at 3.00 p.m., a funeral procession passed slowly up through town, so we all downed tools and followed it, without a word. They must have known, Marie Paz must have known, they all knew a couple of days beforehand that Edwin's Grandmother had died, but nobody had mentioned anything about a funeral to me.

The procession consisted of what seemed to be about half of the community and all of their dogs walking along behind the coffin, which was resting in the back of an old dark blue Japanese estate car as it meandered at a snail's pace, up the dusty rock strewn road between the houses towards the top of the hill on the far side of town. We joined the rear of the procession as it ambled slowly up the main street, to the top of the hill where we stopped outside the gates of the village cemetery on the outskirts of the town. The graveyard rested on the top a very steep rocky, cliff like, escarpment. The view was spectacular, looking down at the greens and browns of the distant valleys below, where the Apurimac River drifted off into the distance, a thin grey line that meandered along the valley floor so far below. The cemetery was enclosed by an old grey stone wall; where lay many tombs, some containing several family members. They were adorned with images and flowers, some fresh and some not so fresh as in any burial ground, and a few adorned with a bottle of cañazo half drunk, by way of celebration, normally if he himself interned, had also been half drunk, or so they told me. They pointed out the occasional bottle and said, "Oh that was Don Peruano, he liked a drink."

We hadn't seen Edwin for quite some time, after being sacked he had been working in the cákras preparing them for cultivation and then, I was told, had been at his grandmother's bedside during her last days. Apparently she had been like a mother to him and he was understandably extremely upset. Edwin had completely lost his normal cool, unforgiving, wide eyed, humorous composure. He cried openly over the coffin at the broad iron gates to the cemetery.

Some of the villagers had brought cases of beer and other beverages such as chicha and cañazo, but no one was drinking. What was amazing to the European eye was that some of the men openly relieved themselves, facing away from the funeral cortege, a few steps from the cemetery walls, whilst the others were waiting just outside, close to the gates.

162

Apuquri sadly had no resident clergy, which is probably why no one went to a Sunday Service the entire time that I was there. This was despite their strong Catholic belief which was in fact combined with a spiritual pagan worship of Pachamama or Mother Earth, Quillamama, Mother Moon and Tayta Inti, Father Sun, where the people believe in the symbiosis between the cosmos and all things upon earth. They believe that Pachamama has a physical and spiritual reality, and it is Mother Earth that nurtures man and so it is important to offer her reciprocation; hence the custom of pouring a little on the earth before and after taking a drink. This culminates in the celebration of "Pago a la Pachamama" that can be translated as "Payment to the Pachamama". This is a rite celebrated every August at the beginning of the agricultural year, by each extended family and carried out by an Andean priest, called a "Paqo" or "Alto Misayoq".

The Catholic belief manifests itself in the Cult of the Saints, which includes the Virgin Mary and Jesus Christ, who although perceived as the God of the Sun, may be recognized in different forms, not as the same Christ but as several brothers. The cult is celebrated at feasts on the day of each particular saint. The day normally consists of mass, a procession, parades, dancing that may have some religious meaning, bull races, evening prayer, and of course, plenty of eating and drinking.

Baptism is considered to be a rite of passage from a savage to becoming someone, who is a Christian. Other rites such as "Holy Communion" or "Confession" are exercised to a much lesser extent.

A wedding in these remote communities consists of two ceremonies, the first being Servinakuy, based on the Quechua tradition. It is a type of test to be passed, or the first stage of marriage, which normally takes place when the couple are still quite young. The second, Casarakuy,[lvi] being the Catholic wedding, happens later.

Another important ritual is the death rite where the dead are buried with their belongings, in the belief that these may be used in the afterlife. They may also wash the deceased's clothes, as a form of purification. On the day of the consecrated to the dead, they also offer food to the deceased, and in Apuquri they offer cañazo.

The traditional Andean rites are performed by a "Paqo", a post normally passed from father to son, following an initiation, known as a "Servicio"; the function of which may vary according to hierarchy dependent upon the name, status and ability of the deceased. The Paqo belongs to a small regional organisation, which is associated with the institution of the Catholic Church, with its all seeing central power base of the Vatican, which spreads its influence throughout the world. The members are viewed with a certain respect, in view of their position; but also with a certain suspicion, in view of the past historical empirical association with the church. It appears that the reason why the two continue to co-exist may be the lack of a centrally organised traditional Andean religion.

The local Andean theology is based on the inherited principle of reciprocity, in the belief of four sins that go against this ideology. They are theft, deceit, laziness and not only incest derived from biological relationships, but also from spiritual relationships.

Due to the Catholic influence, they also believe in the body and spirit. The spirit is however divided in two, the first being anima or breath. They believe that men have four animas and women seven, which relate to health and to the spiritual part of being whilst still alive. The second part of the spirit is the soul, the same entity that separates from the body upon death. It is said that the soul remains on earth for eight days in order to fulfil those tasks left undone, visiting and reminding relatives of their obligations such as financial commitments and appointments. The soul can go to God if the person led a good life, or become an animal, or a bad woman, if that person committed such grievous offences as incest or witchcraft.

The community had hired an Ecclesiastical Priest for the funeral who did not have his own Parish but would travel from one to the other when needed. We waited quietly outside the cemetery walls, while the priest said a few words over the coffin before it was taken in through the gates; this was our signal to leave. We walked slowly back to work in silence, down through the village in the still clean air, along the dusty grey tracks of the streets.

* * *

At the end of the day's labour, slightly later than normal at around 6.00 p.m., we cleared all the tools up and put them in the ancient animal shelter we used as a storeroom just at the top of the site. Juan Carlos turned up as night was falling and we were just finishing up for the day. When everything was in place, we all sat around on the dry straw in the old building, and shared a half litre of what the locals called whisky, which was a mild tasting drink, brown in colour, more akin to a deceptively strong type of rum.

When that bottle had been passed around until it was empty, we walked out across the main square, along one of the adjacent streets to the wake, still in our unkempt building clothes of course. When we arrived we walked through a side gate up into a large, sloped, lawned garden that opened out above of us, behind a large adobe house that faced the plaza. The men walked on and I was invited to sit in the centre of a line of chairs which were placed high on the lawn to overlook proceedings. Food and drinks were offered in the usual way by the more senior ladies in many skirts and everybody was customarily drinking. Marie Paz arrived shortly after we arrived and sat with me, to my left. I was formally introduced to the elder who seemed to be in charge, who sat next to me, to my right. He must have been well into his eighties, was slightly broader and taller than most of the men in the village and had the authoritative air of someone who had some status. We exchanged the normal respectful, pleasantries, which was a custom that I was beginning to become quite accustomed to. It seemed that I was given a place of honour for my help on the project. I didn't really feel as though I had done enough to have been afforded such respect; but I did notice a little of the green eyed monster in the conduct of Juan Carlos, who appeared to be slightly less forthright than was normal.

It became apparent that the senior man was aware of my support over the mining contract. I was in hope that the notes which I had given to Marie Paz one evening were going to be kept confidential until I had left, simply because I didn't want the miners to know that I had been meddling with the contract for the gold extraction rights. If they were discovered by the miners, life could have become incredibly dangerous for me in Apuquri.

As we talked I was introduced to the husband of the poor woman who had died. He was also well into his eighties and was a very dignified man. Edwin's Grandmother had in fact died at eight seven years of age, which was quite young, in comparison to the life expectancy of most of the people in Apuquri, which was incredibly sad. We talked about the community and as the conversation progressed the senior man said, "I say you wouldn't mind awfully siring one of the local girls would you old chap? Only quite frankly old boy we're a tad short on the old blood stock, what?" I said: "That's jolly kind of you to offer, that would an absolute pleasure, you know, anything in support of the community. Did you have anyone in mind perchance?" He said, "No, no, really don't worry about that dear boy, be my guest, I'm sure we could sort out a few for you to choose from." It's not the type of thing one might expect to be asked at a wake, and it was meant in all sincerity. I said that I was extremely complemented, and I would certainly consider his offer.

Marie Paz and I had left fairly early as most of the people at the wake were probably going to continue drinking for quite some time. We did talk quite a lot on occasion, Marie Paz and I. When we had said our farewells, we walked away together back up the hill in the calm serenity of the lustrous star filled night. I told Marie Paz about what the old man had said, and asked her if he was serious, she said, "Oh yes, he's serious alright," I said, "but I am leaving, you know that, and if this were to happen, who would look after the child". She very simply told me "The community will look after it of course," as though that would be no problem at all, to leave a fatherless child for the good of the community would have been perfectly acceptable. Marie Paz didn't seem to mind at all, and if Marie Paz didn't mind at all, it seemed that no one else would mind at all either.

Saturday 19ᵗʰ September

I got to work late, after Marie Paz's usual life giving breakfast, with a very slight hangover. We had drunk a little the night before, and it had its effect; my excuse was it was Saturday, and I was only supposed to work weekdays, which was of course nonsense, considering the amount of time I had taken off, in European terms.

When I got to work Oscar was stood on the lawn at the top of the slope above the site, he had his sleeve rolled up, as he held a Hururunjay by the wings between his fingertips, just above the bare skin of his arm, and he was encouraging it. I said to him "¿Buenas días Oscar, que pasa? ¿Que haces con el Hururunjay? Ten cuidad va a picarte," and he said, "No te preocupes, si me pique, va a curarme de la artritis. La primera vez te da una fiebre, que dura un par de días, pero la segunda o tercera vez, no hay un problema; posiblemente se irritará un poco, nada más." I said, "Pero, por lo momento, no quiero una picadura, como sabes, eres un poco loco, pero entiendo que tienes razon en querer que la abeja te pique" to which Oscar replied, "Así es, pero esta mañana el bastardo no quiere hacerlo".ˡᵛⁱⁱ God we laughed.

I set to work helping Don Moreno and Oscar with the roof trusses which wasn't really what could be described as a demanding job. In fact I probably would still have been happier carrying the bricks, or getting covered in mud or both. Don Moreno was as usual Mr. Cool being tooled up with his chainsaw, which if stood on end, with its elongated blade, was still taller than he was. We collected the longest straightest tree trunks, we then cut the knots down and built about half a dozen triangular roof trusses, each about six metres wide, and two metres tall.

It being a relaxed Saturday, not entirely dissimilar to any other day in fact, having abandoned lunch we stopped work early at around 3.00 p.m. We made a couple of benches out of planks that we had placed on adobe bricks along the inside walls in the largest room of the unfinished, roofless adobe building. We sent Andino to buy some chicha and had only just sat down when Juan Carlos turned up with a bottle of rum, which was convenient because it took the pressure off me to buy yet another jerry can of chicha, when the first would no doubt be finished.

The mood changed from a room full of ridiculous, nonsensical, banter to one of guarded expectation, as Juan Carlos took centre stage. He opened his laptop to play some forgettable music that sounded as though it was being played on a scratched record. Then I realised what all the fuss was about, it was, in simplistic terms, that which changes the minds of men, money. Juan Carlos sat back on one of the benches and with great candour, pulled out a package of light brown envelopes. He then called out the names of each individual worker and handed them a wage packet, which they each signed for in turn. I can only imagine that Marie Paz kept a record of who had worked each day, because I had no idea who would have done it otherwise. The work force was constantly changing and Juan Carlos had normally disappeared, to somewhere in Chalhuanca or Abancay, probably.

I didn't see it with my own eyes but it was rumoured that he was entertaining one of the young local girls on a regular basis and if it were true, it meant that he may have been spending charity money on things that he shouldn't have, like hotel rooms for two.

When all the wages had been handed out, we began to plan the ceremony for the completion of the roof. The house was to be blessed and the religious symbols being crosses, which were to be placed at the apex of the roof. The same can be seen growing from the ridges of the majority of roofs in Peru, in particular in rural areas. I was given the venerated position of Padrino of the Casa Hogar as was Juan Carlos, which seemed a little ironic. It also meant that there would be two crosses. I was extremely proud of the honour, but at the same time, if I am honest, a little disappointed, in fact cross, in view of Juan Carlos's appointment as Padrino. Nonetheless Juan Carlos had done his job, and he had managed the project to the imminent completion of the roof. So fair play to him, as they say. Even if I was somewhat concerned about his conduct, who am I to judge on the ways of the Peruvians? It was clear that the workers thought there was nothing untoward about the normal absence of their esteemed ignoramus of a project manager who had little idea of what he was doing. Hercules had told me, in no uncertain terms, that it took an awful long time to order materials, perhaps he had a valid point.

A few members of the gentler sex arrived a little later on in their many layered skirts and traditional fedoras. Marie Paz turned up as well and we all had a small party, which didn't go on for very long for Marie Paz and me. The presence of the women did create a more conservative atmosphere, as could happen in England or Spain, or anywhere else for that matter in just the same way, though that may have changed when the drink had begun to flow.

* * *

Marie Paz and I had been planning a couple of days off, and were going to leave the following day to go on a trip. We had intended to leave that afternoon but time being what it is in Peru that idea had soon fallen away. So we made a concerted effort and left the bacchanalians to party on into the night while we returned home to pack for the journey.

When we got to the steps below Marie Paz's front door we met Victor and a couple of friends; so as it wasn't so late, we men went for a drink in the store just there opposite Marie Paz's place, while Marie Paz went in to make some supper. The women simply didn't go to bars to drink with the men, but they would have a drink at home or at a fiesta. This was quite old fashioned; however some old traditions do in fact make sense. In some parts of Peru[lviii] the women must walk four or more paces behind the men.

When I got back from the bar, a little worse for wear, Marie Paz had prepared a highly nutritious supper which consisted of a herbal potato soup. It makes you healthy just thinking about it. As soon as supper was over we set about packing our bags for our trip the following day, which was easy because we didn't really have a lot to take.

We actually stayed up until around 10.00 p.m., we discussed the possible fall of the Empire of the Western World over a few glasses of the local throat burner, which was taken with a little coke. That rum was quite useful, I remember that it was brutally cold that night; we could see our breath as we spoke. When it was time to retire I was freezing as I balanced on my shoes once more, in bare feet in the dark, before I climbed under my twelve blankets, naked as the day I was born, I drifted off to sleep in the darkness of the night.

Sunday 20th September

The day dawned clear and bright and Marie Paz and I got up quite early that morning. I finished off packing while Marie Paz knocked up some eggs. Juan Carlos came by to say goodbye, and probably, more to the point, to get some breakfast. We also lent Juan Carlos the ring burners, for cooking while we were away (not the curry sauce type). We were only going to be gone for a couple of days, four at most, which turned out to be quite an optimistic estimate, but then again, what is time in Peru? Perhaps there is more of it.

Marie Paz and I left to walk down into the sun drenched village centre to find a taxi to Chalhuanca at around 8.30 a.m. But there was no one to be found, the place was empty. I figured that it must be because it was a Sunday. I asked Marie Paz what we should do, she said we should walk, I said how long will that take? She said about an hour and a half, down the old path to the Pan-American Highway at the bottom of the valley beneath, from where we would pick up a short taxi ride into Chalhuanca. So, without a hint of disappointment, we decided to walk, because to walk would have been a pleasure. To walk for many miles is something quite normal for the mountain people. Marie Paz told me that they would walk for hours sometimes across the mountains as a matter of course, just to visit friends or family, because more often than not they had no other form of transport. It is ironic that people in Europe spend time weeks in advance planning hiking trips in the mountains, but in the Andes, clearly a trek was an ordinary everyday event.

We were about to leave when suddenly, seemingly from nowhere, another old blue Japanese estate car appeared, along a track from the other side of the village square. The driver pressed his horn a couple of times and more than half a dozen people rapidly emerged from apparently nowhere, and piled into the car. I was given pride of place in the front as usual, whilst what seemed to be most of the village climbed in. We descended the steep sided gravel and rock hewn track, listening to the obligatory Peruvian violin salsa playing on the crackling radio waves. I paid Sol. 20 for Marie Paz and I, which is cheap, but not for Apuquri. I have a sneaking suspicion that again, it was gringo price, which was likely to have been double what the locals pay.

We got to Chalhuanca after a relaxed drive down the rocky mountain road, which was always a bonus; the last person you want to drive along those cliff edged tracks is someone who believes that their true vocation in life was to take on the role of Emerson Fittipaldi.

When we arrived in Abancay we immediately walked up the high street to find a surprisingly immaculate, almost brand new, shiny white people carrier, the large type of carrier which are used as minibuses in that part of the world. We climbed in to go to Abancay, a major metropolis about one hour away, en route towards our final destination. These minibuses are a good cheap method of transport, known locally as colectivos; each passenger pays for a seat as is normal however there is a slight difference to most other bus services, in that there is no timetable. Consequently, to make his journey worthwhile the driver will drive around town until he has found enough people to fill the minibus and then go merrily on his way. That day was no exception and fortunately for me, I quite like Chalhuanca, and as luck

173

would have it, that particular morning we were provided with a tour of the town. However after half an hour there was nothing much else to see, even though it is the capital of the county, it is a very small town with a population of only 1,000.

It took at least two circuits of Chalhuanca before the driver had filled a sufficient number of seats for the trip. We eventually found ourselves underway along the main road to Abancay which is as good a road as any that might be found in Europe. It sweeps alongside the river, beneath the spectacular rocky outcrops, flecked with greenery, that rise almost vertically, a few hundred metres above the river valley floor.

We drove for an hour or so until the river gorge opened out into Abancay, a town of approximately 58,000 residents, situated in a broad valley at 2,378m above sea level. Chalhuanca is a hamlet in comparison. Abancay is a market town set mainly on a grid system where remnants of the Spanish colonial empire can be seen in the centre of a town that spreads out towards the fertile slopes that lead up to the forested heights of the snow-capped mountains that look down upon the town. The streets bustle with traders whose shops flow out onto the charming, sometimes covered, cobbled walkways. There is also a large enclosed market, common to Peruvian towns, which sells all manner of fresh, predominantly organic food. As they often do, that day the paisanos[lix] had descended from their mountain hideaways to sell their rustic goods that they lay out on blankets before them, in the surrounding streets.

We walked away from the bustling markets up into the periphery of the commercial centre, where we found ourselves a Chinese restaurant for lunch, in much the same way as might be found in any European city. Chinese restaurants can be found in most South American cities where there is often a rich varied menu of rice and noodle dishes. The food is usually extremely tasty and they are normally very good value. Following an incredibly pleasant lunch of Arroz Chaufa,[ix] we walked downtown into an internet café, close to the old colonial Spanish Plaza. We needed to adjust whatever needed to be adjusted in the outside world, which included a gentle reminder of the appeal to the charity in England for the alteration of the roof design of the Casa Hogar. Fortunately for me though, someone had sent me another link.

We then meandered up through the inclined streets; Marie Paz asked where we might find a colectivo to take us up into what turned out to be a distant mountain village, known as Huanicapa. We were reliably informed that we would find one a few blocks towards the top of town, away from the commercial centre. We walked up the slopes, through the clean urban streets, where the view of the valley opened up before us. By what seemed a complete coincidence we came upon a house with a dusty grey walled yard beside it, where the obligatory dark blue Japanese estate car was about to leave for Huanicapa, our chosen destination for the night. It seems that whatever we needed became a reality, one thing quite simply flowed into another.

We climbed into the taxi, I was given the front seat of the car which we shared with three of the locals and fortunately we left almost immediately. We drove up through the narrow city streets out onto the wide, well maintained, modern roads that sweep up into the mountains. We rapidly achieved heights that I had never imagined, that looked down upon the city. As dusk came upon us, we passed fewer and fewer cars until suddenly, without warning, we turned upwards, off the clean metalled road to take a potholed, single file, gravel track. It wended its way along shallow valleys, to rock hewn roadways cut into the mountain side, so high that we could look down upon the clouds that rested in the darkened gorges beneath us. It was not the most comfortable feeling as the night fell upon us, the humidity turned and the rain began to fall. Visibility was low as we passed through the rolling mist, while the car bounced over the potholes along the edge of cliffs that dropped down into the depths of obscurity hundreds of meters beneath us.

We arrived at Huanicapa at around 7.00 p.m. after a cold, dark and wet, two hour drive. The town was seemingly untouched by the rain and was quite warm and dry. It was incredibly isolated; it had a really old fashioned atmosphere, as though it was untouched by the modern world. Huanicapa was a very small unkempt place, about the same size as Apuquri, possibly smaller. It had a primitive, poverty stricken air about it, to such a degree that it made Apuquri seem positively cosmopolitan by comparison. The town was built around an old dilapidated, grey stone colonial Spanish Plaza that must have been around five hundred years old. A step or so down from the edge of the plaza, on two sides, were a few grocery shops selling basic provisions; there was an old hotel or two adjacent set back from the square with little or no facade. The focal point was a rustic restaurant, come bar, which was bustling with local people, who sat around drinking bottles of beer playing cards or quite simply enjoying the company of the people around them.

We asked around and were directed to an ancient hotel built just back from the main square that consisted of two stories of rooms, the upper floor with a balcony, built around a narrow inner quadrangle. The cost was Sol. 10 (£2) a night per person, so we booked separate rooms for the night. There were showers, that were really cold but refreshing nonetheless and flushing loos that you could sit on. This to me was luxury, particularly after so many Englishman's washes and the only loo for the past couple of weeks having been nothing more than a hole in the ground, covered by a corrugated tin roof. But sadly I couldn't wave to the neighbours.

When we had both settled in and had freshened up for the evening, Marie Paz and I walked out into the main square to the popular bar to get some food. I remember the yellow lighting illuminated everything in the bar which was incredibly arcadian in character. When we walked in I felt a sense that the locals were not particularly friendly, they were clearly not used to strangers, an atmosphere that was not entirely dissimilar to certain pubs in Wales, or indeed the Yorkshire Dales. It was interesting how different the character of each village could be. The bar was very busy, the people were quite vibrant and they seemed, for some unknown reason, to be physically larger than other people I have seen in Peru. It was the kind of place you might expect to meet Hiram Bingham, this was exciting. They looked at us with a certain nonchalance, almost disdain, it was as though they had no real interest in us at all, which was quite unusual, I had never before sensed that in Peru.

We sat down at one of the small wooden tables and ordered, from the very limited menu, what turned out to be a rather, meagre, greasy chicken and chips. It would not have been out of place in a basket in a pub in England in the 1980's, with room to spare. I had a large dark beer, and the whole meal came to the princely sum of Sol. 21.50 (+/-£4). This must have been Gringo price.

Huanicapa was a convenient place to stay the night en route to our final destination, which was an ancient, long since deserted Inca city known as Choquekiraw[lxi] which is part of a network of ancient Andean conurbations, situated high up in the Andes which are connected to Machu Picchu. It is certain that some of this group of interconnected cities remain hidden, unknown to this day, beneath the semi tropical jungle of the region. Announcements are made of new discoveries in certain parts of Peru almost every year.

Machu Picchu itself was announced to the Western World by an American explorer named Hiram Bingham, on 24 July 1911. Some say that it is the greatest archaeological discovery to date. Some say that this city was built high in the mountains to escape from the oppression of the Spanish Conquista of the early 1500's. This doesn't make sense, as is often true of what is written about South America, by historians foreign to the continent. The focal point of the citadel of Machu Picchu is an observatory, it was a place of learning, and that level of civilisation could not have been born in a day; it seems illogical to suggest that it was not developed over quite some time. It is far more likely that the city is well over five hundred years old, that may have still have many hidden treasures, such as an ancient cemetery that may rest beneath it.

There have been relatively sophisticated societies in Peru for centuries, some of which are pyramid cities that evidence suggests are more than five thousand years old. According to custom, many people had wanted to live in the sierras, where they lived in polyphony with the stars, they wanted to live close to the heavens, they wanted to be close to their gods and they believed in the harmonious synergy between man and the astrological cycles of the universe.[lxii]

Throughout the ancient civilisations, in South America and in the rest of the world, there lies a common thread, the cities were built in alignment with the movement of the sun and the moon and the stars. There must have been some reason for that, there is something it seems, that has long been forgotten.

* * *

Following our arrival at Huanicapa, Marie Paz and I really didn't know what the next stage of our journey should be. Marie Paz had a rough idea of where we should be going but that was all. I had a sneaking suspicion that descriptive inaccuracy was not entirely uncommon within certain Peruvians, and I was about to have that notion reinforced.

We asked the barmaid, come waitress, in the plaza bar, if she knew anything of Choquekiraw. She reliably informed us, over a discussion of what must have been half an hour, that her son had been there many times, she made it sound as though Choquekiraw was his second home, she gave the impression that he was there almost every other day. She seemed quite disappointed that her son couldn't guide us, but he had school next day. Nonetheless she said that we would be there in only two or three hours from Huanicapa. She told us we needed to get a taxi the following morning down to the Valle de los Lorros,[lxiii] and from a hotel there, surprisingly called "Hotel de los Lorros"[lxiv] it would only take a two hour hike to get to the lost city of Choquekiraw. She said the archaeological site wasn't very big and could be explored in an afternoon, without any difficulty at all.

We were reliably informed that we could therefore take the half hour taxi, do the two hour hike, spend the day at the city and be back the following evening. We paid the bill and bought provisions from a couple of the shops around the square. The shops sold fresh homemade bread rolls from huge wicker baskets, covered by a cloth. Vegetables and pulses were readily available and there was an abundant array of tin cans on the shelves, so we acquired tinned tuna fish, onion, a little cheese, tomatoes, bread rolls etc. and all for only Sol. 5.20 (£1.05).

When we retired to the Hotel at 10.00 p.m. it seemed that the whole town was still awake, which was unusual for a place so small. It seemed that no one cared for any particular time to get to bed. The square was busy with people and the shops remained open until quite gone midnight. It wasn't that it was late by any means according to European standards, but it was something that we were not accustomed to in such an isolated environment. In Apuquri there was no such night life, the town was asleep quite early, and there was focal point to socialise, there was no bar in Apuquri in the colonial plaza, in which to gather. Ironically this is a failing elsewhere, despite the movies, there are few such focal points throughout the United States.

My room at the hotel was perfectly adequate but it was quite scruffy and sparse; there wasn't even the customary picture of the Virgin Mary hanging on a wall. The dark orange walls were flaking in places; it clearly hadn't seen a lick of paint for quite some time. I had a single bed with little bedding, so I slept in my sleeping bag that night under the only blanket provided. It was cold but I was quite comfortable, it had electric light and it was still a blessing to be able to sit down on the communal loo, albeit behind a flimsy curtain that was the door; but nonetheless somewhat less social than Apuquri when in "flagrante delicto", as it were. The courtyard was pleasant, with its few plants in pots arranged in a haphazard way around the walls and some washing hanging from the upper balconies. It had a certain old world charm about it.

I set my alarm for 5.00 a.m., when I settled in to sleep at around 11.00 p.m.

Monday 21st September

I slept right through and woke got up in the cold at 5.00 a.m. I got up and took a freezing shower and packed my rucksack, which I was going to leave in the hotel. Marie Paz and I were only going to need a small bag for our relatively brief excursion.

When we had completed our ablutions we walked into the village to look for a place to buy some breakfast. Luckily we found a charming little place that was about to open on the corner of one of the side streets, a block or so up from the main square. After a few minutes wait we were eventually allowed in, at shortly before 6.00 a.m. We ordered a breakfast which consisted of two fried eggs and bread, Marie Paz ordered a café solo and I, a café con.[lxv] We were each provided with a mug of black coffee and I was told that I would have to wait a few minutes for the milk, which didn't seem unreasonable. The eggs and the bread were very agreeable and much needed. The milk arrived a few minutes later in the form of a large glassful, still warm, provided directly from a cow, a few blocks down the street. Such is the nature of café con leche in that isolated part of the world and all for Sol. 4.5 or (90p) for two, I certainly know how to treat a lady.

We stocked up on a few more provisions from the shops in the plaza and after some searching and intense negotiation we a found a taxi, which would take us down to the Hotel de los Lorros that morning and bring us back in the evening, the cost for the return for the day, was Sol. 60 (£12). This was very expensive for that part of the world, in particular because a labourer earns Sol. 25 (£5) a day and a skilled artisan earns Sol. 50 (£10) a day. This was so expensive, it must have been that the driver would take the journey twice. Clearly he wouldn't wait for us all day, doing nothing until the evening, to take us back to the village, or so I thought.

We drove out of town through the dusty rustic streets, lined with broken down old adobe houses painted in once splendid, weather worn, whitewash. When we left the environs of the town, a stunning broad open lush green valley opened out before us, the Valle de los Lorros is probably one of the most beautiful places I have ever seen. The sparsely populated, well managed green pastures flowed down from the mountains and had only the very occasional farmhouse dotted amongst them; the snow-capped peaks looked down upon us in magnificent grandeur. Apart from the occasional car, the few people we saw were walking or riding on horseback, for what must have been for quite some distance; it must have been at least an hour's drive to the Hotel. The local people travelled at a contented leisurely pace, they were in no hurry, the Andean people take great pleasure in the slow pace of life. We stopped and gave a lift to a couple of schoolchildren who were walking a few miles to a school which consisted of only two buildings, that were situated almost in the centre of the valley, miles from anywhere. When we arrived at the gates I was quite surprised when out of the blue the children gave us Sol. 5 for their ride as they got out of the car. I wasn't expecting any money, I guess in retrospect I should have given it back, but to my shame, I didn't. It was all so sudden, I barely had time to say "Muchas Gracias" or "bacon sandwich" for that matter, before they had departed, which is really no excuse at all.

The wide open fields of the valley flowed down to a small dirt road, where the road narrowed to a single track, bordered by high verdant hedges, it was just wide enough to fit a car. After a mile or so, as the valley floor diminished, the track led us to the Hotel de los Lorros. We pulled up to the walled, black steel gated hotel at around 9.00 a.m., after what had been over an hour's drive. We asked the driver to stay a few moments while we confirmed the time for the return journey. We waited several minutes in the heat of the sun, the day was warming up. After a couple of minutes, a young woman, a proprietor of the hotel, opened the metal door within one side of the large black steel gate. It was a smart, well-kept place, well presented to cater for the well healed tourist, but entirely empty. It had an uncomplicated garden that lead down to a small river that followed the line of the road, along the far side of the lawn. The majority of the available rooms were within the hotel building itself; however there were also a few grey stone chalets for hire, set back away from the main building.

The Italian woman, who welcomed us, was in her mid-thirties, quite slim and well presented in her modest shoes, jeans and her brief dark brown leather jacket. She had a slightly untoward manner about her; she was surprisingly officious in her conduct, bordering on antipático, this was quite strange for a hotel proprietor.

We told her of our plan to trek to Choquekiraw that morning, and return that evening; we wondered what time we should ask the taxi driver to come back to collect us. She said that it was at least six hours to get to the lodge at the Apurimac River, which stood at the base of a climb that would rise over 1000 metres to get to the city. This would take a trek of a minimum of a further five hours. Then when

184

we did arrive at Choquekiraw, we should at least spend a whole day there. It was then that her shaven headed Italian husband came in from tending the field opposite and substantiated what his wife was saying. On a table in reception, there was a large, incredibly accurate model of the mountain region that we were in, which they promptly used to illustrate exactly the route to the lost city that we were planning to visit.

This was not the most uplifting information. The journey was no longer a short hike, but a two day trek. It shouldn't have, but it became a daunting prospect, even though this was the trip of a lifetime. We were going into the unknown and we were not well prepared for such a long hike. It rapidly became apparent that we had to go back up to Huanicapa to collect our sleeping bags, and rucksacks. We then had to return down the valley to the Hotel de los Lorros to continue on our way, to spend the night at the lodge at the Bridge over the River Apurimac, which was a pain in the proverbial. We would then need to continue the next morning, to ascend to the vertiginous heights where Choquekiraw could be found. We needed to chance the journey even though we had little idea of where we were going and we were seriously lacking in equipment.

The waitress in the bar the night before had clearly been talking absolute nonsense, but then again she probably wanted us to be happy, so she simply told us what she thought we wanted to hear, which had little to do with reality. What we had thought was to be a simple excursion had now become a journey that was now going to take considerably longer than anticipated and I didn't really want to be away from the works of the Casa Hogar for quite so much a time.

We got into the taxi and drove back up to town, having decided that the trek to Choquekiraw was an opportunity not to be missed. When we arrived back at Huanicapa, we asked the driver to wait while we collected our things, and then to return to the Hotel de los Lorros. We thought he understood that instead of returning that evening he was merely going back immediately. How wrong we were, the driver insisted that his work was done and he wanted me to pay him Sol. 60 for the journey so far and another Sol. 60 to do the return journey. I argued with him vehemently over this. Marie Paz was very quiet, it soon became apparent that I had better pay, or the situation could become quite ugly. It was clearly "take advantage of the Gringo time". He continued to demand Sol. 60, which I knocked down on principle. I paid him Sol. 50 and left in disgust, after having thrown the money on the ground at his feet. Marie Paz told me to be careful; this could be dangerous, we did not after all, know how the village people might react in this distant place. Rule number one: Don't get obstreperous with the locals. Rule number two: Don't get obstreperous with the locals.

We then had a little luck, we found a thoroughly decent fellow in the marketplace at the edge of the central plaza. He gave us the return journey to the Hotel de los Lorros in yet another dilapidated Japanese estate car, this one was a rather dull silver colour, in place of the normal dark blue. This time we paid the normal fare of Sol. 30.

We got back down to the Hotel de Los Lorros at shortly after 11.00 a.m., the driver gave us his phone number and agreed to come and collect us in a couple of days. The Italian lady reminded us of our journey using the seemingly authentic model of the area, and implied that not much equipment was needed; she lent us a small tent which made

186

our bags heavier, and we left some of our luggage with her, which clearly made our bags lighter. We said our farewells and began our six hour hike, down the valley towards the river lodge. At first it was quite intimidating to know that we were going so far outside our normal comfort zone, which in my case, had recently been extended to the mountains of Apuquri, but that apprehension soon drifted away as we began our gradual decent alongside the narrow river, down along the beautiful Valle de los Lorros.

It is hard to describe the beauty of the valley, miles from anywhere, no civilization in sight, walking down a dusty camino on the way to a lost city in the Andes.

At first we followed the same small dirt road that narrowed further as it entered some woodland, a mile or so from the hotel; from where we crossed a narrow wooden bridge that lead into a bridle track. We passed by a family who seemed to be building the straw roof of a small adobe house situated a few yards the pathway aside some trees. The whole family waved, and shouted "Hola!" They seemed very pleased to see us as we passed by on what was a beautiful sunny day, where only a perfect, light breeze washed over us.

As we walked out of the woods, the track began to rise high along the side of steep river gorge, we rounded a bend after a couple of hours and saw ahead of us a huge snow-capped mountain range where a thin grey line could be seen zigzagging up the side of the lush green mountainside at the end of the valley several miles away in the distance. That steep grey mountain path was the Inca camino that we would lead us to Choquekiraw the following day.

After some time we stopped by a freshwater stream that crossed the path, which led into the river in the gorge below.

We drank from the steam and filled our water bottles. We ate a few biscuits as we sat on a wooden bench close by. It was a beautiful calm, tranquil place, the valley was a lush fertile green, the river flowed along the gorge beneath us, the birds were singing, we were miles from anywhere, there was no building in sight, there was no sound from a road; we were in another world.

It was however getting quite warm, the insects were beginning to get lively and unfortunately we had forgotten the repellent. But as luck would have it, Marie Paz spotted a bush that would act as a natural repellent, we pulled the leaves from it to rub on our bare skin and it seemed to work, it was actually quite soothing. We then filled a couple of small bags with the plant leaves for the oncoming journey. Marie Paz also gave me some other leaves she had found to put under my baseball cap to cool my head.

We walked on and met a young Spanish man and his local guide sitting astride mules riding up the pathway, upon return from the long trek to Choquekiraw, they were a welcome sight to see in such a remote place. We exchanged a few pleasantries and they continued along the way.

The sun was beating down upon us, and it was becoming quite hot. It was not until around 4.00 p.m. that we finally found the welcome shade of the semi-tropical jungle that spread around us; at last we had some respite from the heat of the day. As we walked on under the trees, we suddenly came upon avocados, oranges and lemons lying on the pathway. We could also see papaya and mango hanging from the trees that were growing close to the pathway. We gathered some of the fruit together and filled our bags as much as we could. The abundance of fruit was a real luxury; this was not something that could be found in the sparse hills around Apuquri. I realised that these fruits of the earth were not something that were readily available to Marie Paz.

We continued walking down the pathway for a couple of hundred yards, to find the remains of quite a large derelict, roofless, adobe building which we later discovered was what had been an old, a very old, farmhouse. We passed by the aged dilapidated walls of the farmhouse and came upon La Casa de San Ignacio at around 4.30 p.m. La Casa[lxvi] consisted of a group of five or six purpose built light grey, single story hostels, built further down the slope beneath the ruins of the old farmhouse, in amongst the semi tropical forest. La Casa had been financed by the government to promote tourism in the area. However, as yet it had not been an overwhelming success, the place was empty, there was no one around.

It had been a relatively easy walk down a gentle slope to this point and I felt much better. I was glad to have found our destination for the night, but I wasn't so pleased though, to find the place deserted, and there didn't seem to be any mains electricity.

Suddenly from nowhere appeared a small dark haired, wiry man of around fifty years of age. He name was José, the caretaker, a very amenable man who was quite pleased to see us. We were very pleased when he gave us some freshly squeezed orange juice, there were several orange filled boxes in a kitchen at the rear of one of the buildings. That orange juice truly tasted of nectar, if there really is a god, this was a sign. He then shared a couple of glasses of rum with us from the customary single glass, and we rolled a couple of cigarettes from the dried tobacco that he had grown himself, which was actually a very pleasant smoke.

I know this seems crazy, but we realised then and told José, that we had arrived with very little food. We were somewhat relieved when he told us that there was plenty; he said that we should look around the old ruins and take what we could find. There were a few tomatoes, some papas (potatoes), bananas, mangos, papaya and not least by any means, chicken eggs. Before we embarked on our search we gorged ourselves on some more orange juice from the plentiful supply, it was so good it was irresistible.

Marie Paz and I walked through the undergrowth around the remnants of the old farmhouse and took a few tomatoes, potatoes, and papaya. We knocked some bananas down with a long pole, from some tall banana trees that we found growing close behind the house. Some of the bananas had had the tops bitten off by what seemed to be the beaks of the many green parrots that we had seen in pandemonium flying around the place, through the trees along the valley.

When we showed the half eaten bananas to José, he told us that they had not been bitten by parrots, as we had thought, but by the giant fruit bats that live in the forest. He told us that there were plenty of fruit and vampire bats, deer, racoons, bears and snakes that lived in the jungle around us, but not to worry, the bears will normally run away when we see some en route tomorrow, as they mostly eat fruit, not people, just be careful of the snakes. Some comfort that was, to a man who had never seen a bear in the wild, namely me.

As dusk passed by, the cool of nightfall rapidly came upon us, as did a beautiful vista of the night sky. The stars are so incredibly beautiful in that part of the world, there is no light pollution. The stars shine so brightly, and the Milky Way filled the sky. If Patrick Moore hadn't experienced that, I would have gladly raised his airfare.

Marie Paz was absolutely brilliant; she quietly made a wood fire in the garden at the back of the kitchen and cooked us all a tuna and onion supper with papas. We had masses of bright orange papaya to follow, accompanied by a little homemade rum, provided by José. There was no electric light so we set up a candle enclosed by the top half of an upturned two litre plastic bottle. As we sat around the table eating our fabulous candlelit supper, the two dogs that accompanied José, suddenly jumped up and began to bark at the forest like mad things; they ran off into the shaded darkness beneath the trees that surrounded us. It was a bear, a bear, a bloody great big bear that had smelt our food and had decided to come and join us for dinner. The dogs came back after a couple of minutes and we thought the bear was gone, and then suddenly the dogs were off again. I grabbed my torch and caught two red eyes reflected in the beam no more than ten metres away from our supper. However the bear was soon gone again, those eyes disappeared into the darkness of the forest once more, the dogs had finally seen it off. I became rapidly very fond of those two, slight but fearless dogs.

José told us that we would probably see deer and bears that might cross the path en camino the next day; he reassured us once more that the bears really shouldn't present us with any problem. He also told us about how years before his father had been working in the mountains and sleeping in a large workman's tent, when a Vampire bat had bitten him at night, and how that was the manner in which his father had come to lose one of his ear lobes. José told us that we should make sure our toes were covered whilst we slept, because it had been known for the bats to enter the rooms and take a little blood, from the toes or any skin not

191

covered. I was to sleep in a sleeping bag and to be honest the idea of having a Vampire bat having a taste of my earlobe didn't faze me at all, it seemed so unlikely. That is if, in fact, José was telling the truth, there is after all, a certain poetic license in much of what is said in Peru.

We retired at around 8.30p.m. and walked by torchlight to the incredibly large high ceilinged, airy, dormitory rooms which were quite eerie in their emptiness. The dormitories had tiled floors, which was a luxury in comparison to what I had become used to in Apuquri. They also had comfortable twin beds in each room and en suite showers and sinks, quite well set up for the wealthy tourist, but we had to use torchlight, because sadly there was no mains electricity, or hot water for that matter. Marie Paz took one room and I another, next door, and we settled down to sleep. I remember Marie Paz seemed to be incredibly coy that evening; I only hoped that I didn't snore too much.

It was bitterly cold that night, but I soon rolled out my sleeping bag on one of the pair of single beds in my room and I slept like a baby.

Tuesday 22nd September

The alarm went off in the cold crisp obsidian night at 2.30 a.m. I got up reluctantly in the dark, had a freezing cold shower and packed my rucksack by torchlight. I left the tent that the Italians had lent us behind at the lodge. It was heavy and I expected to be back the following evening, I was wrong of course. When I stepped out of my room I looked up and admired the brilliance of the night sky once more, unfettered by electric light. There was silence all around me as I walked around to where we had eaten the night before. Marie Paz was already preparing our breakfast of eggs and papas.

Marie Paz was a god send, probably quite literally.

By the time we had everything ready and we had eaten, we began our descent at 4.30 a.m. which was rather later than we had intended. However we were still beneath the clear still, dark chill of night, with the maze of stars shining brightly above us. We walked down a sloping path through the buildings onto what became a steep rocky mountain path; the gravel underfoot was quite slippery at times. Dawn broke after we had walked for an hour or so, down to the broad wooden suspension bridge that spread out across the Apurimac River at the bottom of the gorge.

We arrived at the river Apurimac at around 5.30 a.m. situated adjacent to the bridge above the deserted, well facilitated, modern lodge of La Playa de San Ignacio[lxvii]. It was of the same design as that where we had stayed the night before, and it was quite eerie in its emptiness.

I was glad of the light of day, the cool of the night lifted as the warm sunlight blazed upon us. We crossed the broad wooden slatted suspension bridge beneath its concrete towers, the deep opaque, rapid waters churning beneath us. The ascent began quite steeply at the other side; we were soon several hundred feet up along the cliff side pathway, jumping across gaps where the earth had fallen away. The climb was quite unnerving as the drop to our right hand side was so steep; the ground was again slippery underfoot, it was covered in loose rocks and gravel.

We ascended in the mosquito, sand fly heat, the sun was rising, the temperature was mounting, and the flies became more persistent. I began to wish that I had remembered the insect repellent. The plant remedy gave some respite, but it seemed that it was not nearly as good as a bottle of Ben's Tick and Insect Repellent with 30% Deet, available at all good Insect Repellent Stores. There are other repellents available.

We rapidly gained height; in places the narrow path was really quite precarious. The drop by my side was nothing more than certain death, a fall of hundreds of feet with no barrier. Vertigo kicked in, my mind began to play tricks on me, it would be so easy to jump. I decided not to look over the edge for a while, I turned my head down as I walked, to stare at the security of the path to my left away from the cliff. The fear came in waves, I had to fight the illogical perturbation. I had to explain to myself that the angst I felt had no reason; it was merely that I wasn't used to the height of the cliffs. After some time the waves of apprehension subsided and began to slow down. Marie Paz carried on a few paces ahead, I could not allow myself to show any fear or trepidation in any way.

Following a hike of a good couple of hours, we had achieved some altitude; the gorge fell beneath us over what seemed to be a drop of several hundred metres of scrub strewn rock. After some time we arrived at some abrupt stone steps cut into the mountainside, they were quite unnerving to say the least, the sheer drop over the edge was quite spectacular, there was no barrier whatsoever and the sheer vertical side to the steps gave no false impression as to quite how high we were.

As we climbed we arrived at the occasional vista, where stone benches had been made, resting beneath vertical rock faces looking down upon the valley below. We stopped to take in the spectacular view; we sat upon a cliff edge that was so high, it was like looking out of an aeroplane. On occasion we walked through tunnels made through the semi tropical jungle. We came across the occasional ancient stone wall on the way. That made the journey magical, knowing that this trail had been trodden for a thousand years or more. I could imagine the Inca walking along this path as though it were a Sunday stroll, it was beautiful. The height and the fatigue on occasion created some considerable anxiety within me but it was certainly a far better day out than shopping in Basingstoke[lxviii] on a Saturday afternoon.

We walked and walked, we kept on walking. After eight or so hours, and we didn't seem to be particularly slow, I was hot and sweating, I was bitten by sand flies, I was exhausted, I wondered when it would ever end. We passed through what had become a semi-tropical jungle; many times we thought we were almost at our destination, only for the deceptive bends to prove us wrong again and again.

We hiked and hiked up that veering, slippery gravel slope until at around 4.30 p.m., through the trees, we saw, from our tree lined pathway, rising from the jungle beneath, some amazing perfectly aligned, symmetrical, stone terraces in the valley to our right. All hope was in sight, we saw a brown ring tailed racoon cross the path, the only animal that had had the grace to show itself all day, perhaps this was a sign. In fact it turned out to be a new species of racoon, which was discovered the following year.

Eventually, after following many undulating paths through the dry warmth of the semi tropical jungle, high up on the mountain, we arrived at the high slopes of the ancient city at around 5.40 p.m. We stepped out of the forest onto the grass lawn pathway that rested above the highest of a series of grey stone walled terraces that stepped down beneath us. We had arrived at a fantastic vantage point that looked down upon the valley so far below. We had finally reached part of the city that had been cleared from beneath the jungle. The well-kept terraces led to a couple of modern shower buildings, such as you might find on any campsite, except that they sat on top of the world over looking (only) part of an Inca city that could be anything over a 1000 years old, if not more, no one really knows how old Choquekiraw is. A few yards further on were the washing facilities, and then there was a rangers' hut, where they stayed from time to time, to monitor the coming and going of the tourists, and to assist in the clearance work and maintenance of the site.

There was hardly anyone else there, possibly four tents at first, placed in a neat row at the end of the grass covered terrace. A little later on a group of half a dozen hikers appeared, who were from England; they were spending six or seven days in the mountains and had walked from Machu Picchu. They placed their tents in a neat line along the lawned terrace a few steps from the wash house and were in high spirits. They told me that they had seen a few other small abandoned settlements on what had been a spectacular hike over the past few of days.

As we sat down on the grass terrace wondering what we were going to do, Dayme, a 6ft tall, Peruvian guy, of around 60 years of age, arrived from seemingly nowhere and introduced himself to us; by chance we were sitting close to the remains of his previous night's fire. He was a top man, in more than one sense, as fit as you like, he worked as a guide and was completely at home in the mountains, in fact he was a mountaintop man. He was the guide on this occasion to two French girls and a young Frenchman. He was more than happy to help us out when he realised that we had no idea what we were going to eat or where we were to sleep. It was a great relief when he told us that he would find us a place where we could spend the night, and would provide us with some food. If I had had the choice, which I did, it would not have been to climb up a mountain to a lost city in the mountains with no food; that would not be the most sensible or indeed intelligent thing to do.

As the sun went down, at around 7.00 p.m., we collected some wood and made a fire on the ancient terrace. Dayme began to boil up some incredibly nourishing chocolate soup, with some kind of wheat mixed in. It was then that two extremely attractive French girls arrived, one a midwife in Cuzco, the other a medical student. Their friend Pascal, a young Frenchman, then came to join us. Pascal had also been working in Cuzco, he was assisting in the hospital there. He and the girls had employed Dayme for a few days. He told me how he was helping out in the hospital for no pay, as part of his training and how Cuzco was a party town, where drugs were rife. At which point he produced a joint, which we shared, and we got higher than we were already. It seemed as though we were sat on the Pink Fairies' *Never Never Land* album cover, with our feet dangling over the edge of a planet, overlooking the universe, looking out into the haze of the Milky Way and the bright sparkling Peruvian stars above us, with the shadows of the mountains all around us. I didn't inhale of course.

We shared the chocolate soup and sat around telling stories until the French party departed to their respective tents at around 11.00 p.m. and Dayme took us up a pathway into the darkness, through the woods up behind the top of the terraces. We walked along the undulating trail by the light of the stars, tripping occasionally. We only used the torchlight momentarily, when absolutely necessary, because Dayme did not want us to be seen by the Rangers. Dayme was a fast walker and I was embarrassed because it was difficult to keep up with this sixty year old man, especially as we were at such altitude, and the air was so thin. Eventually after a fifteen minute hike we arrived at a group of old labourer's empty huts that had been used to house the workmen when they had first come to clear the ruins beneath the jungle.

The huts stood atop a slope that overlooked the terraces from a few hundred yards on the opposite side. We chose a hut at random, which we had to enter without using any torchlight. It was full of bunk beds in neat aligned order; it was incredibly dusty, and incredibly dry. It reminded me of Hollywood horror stories where the innocent students find an old disused building in the woods, in the middle of nowhere and decide to use it as shelter for the night. But unbeknown to them a raving axe murderer has been watching their every move, whilst wearing the skin of their friend who had mysteriously disappeared the day before;

following their every move, as they meandered, lost, afraid and hungry through the mountainous woods. I digress.

While the others lay down to sleep, I stepped outside to look across the vale towards the huge stepped Inca terraces, and way down the steep valley to where the mighty river Apurimac flowed, more than a kilometre beneath us. The deep, dark blue sky was magnificent; it shone above the silhouette of the distant peaks. The Milky Way was so rich and the stars so vivid, there is no comparison to that sight I have seen anywhere else in the world. I could understand why the Inca had become such incredible astronomers, and how they were understood to have chosen to live so high in the mountains to be closer to the spirit of their Gods. They believed that we are merely a field of energy that moves upon this earth in the form of man, and how the intrinsic entity of our being, our soul, will never die, and so did I.

I finished my cigarette in the stillness of the night and walked around the side of the hut to relieve myself. Suddenly, I heard something large move in the dense woodland beside me. I froze, a shiver drifted down my spine.

Wednesday 23rd September

I awoke at 5.00 a.m. lying on a bottom bunk bed, a name which sounds as though it were designed for a particular activity. In the light of day the hut revealed just how dingy it was, there were four rows of four or five old wooden bunk beds, everything was covered in dust and cobwebs. I got out of there as quickly as I had gone in, the breath of the clean air and the sunshine outdoors, came with some relief.

Marie Paz of course was already up, awake and outside. Dayme was long since gone and had left us the blankets we slept in to take back for him, to Abancay. They were somewhat of a burden, I could see why he wanted us to carry them, but that was no problem at all, Dayme, had after all been incredibly generous.

It was a beautiful sunny day; the air was still, with only the wisp of a cloud resting in the vale beneath us. We walked back through the woods to where the fire had been the night before; the place was deserted apart from a couple of small two man tents. The well-ordered English row of tents had long since disappeared. I walked back to the showers, took a drink of water and filled a couple of plastic bottles that we had procured.

We then walked back up into the woods to see what we could explore of the city. It was very well signed and there was the occasional map to show the tourist where he or she was. It was still, nonetheless, easy to get completely lost in the woodland trails that lead to the various sites that had been uncovered. Marie Paz and I roughly planned a round trip and walked up through the steep wooded pathways to what was believed to have been Administrative Centre Building Sector IV or in other words the Ancient Inca Civil Service Headquarters.

There was no one around in that misty morning except until a young German guy arrived from nowhere. He was travelling alone, but very well decked out in his perfectly styled, and ordered, light weight clothing specifically designed for hiking. He seemed to be a young man who typified the phrase "alles ist in ordnung".[lxix] It turned out that he was studying Law in Spanish, which is a rare skill and quite some coincidence to say the least, as I did that myself. He was working in Cuzco to gain some South American experience and was quite frankly, a thoroughly pleasant chap.

It was absolutely awe inspiring to me to experience those buildings in the city of Choquekiraw. It was built in the same architectural style as Machu Pichu, but was apparently between six and eight times the size. Choquekiraw was more of a functional city that was linked to the city of Machu Pichu, which is said to have been a scholarly centre, almost like a University town, where there was a great observatory, where astronomy was studied in some depth, as though it were the Oxford or Cambridge of the Inca Empire. Choquekiraw itself has only really begun to be uncovered since the early nineteen eighties, when it was rediscovered. It is in such a mountainous region that there are no roads that could lead to the city and it is said that it will take until 2060 to reveal the whole of the city in all its glory. Which is a fair estimate but it is in Peru and there are still many such cities yet to be found.

---

* * *

I do not believe, as the European and North American historians tell us, that the Inca had no written language. We know they had a system of recording volume and detailed accounts. This was in the form of bunches of coloured strings with strategically placed knots, known as "Quipus". We also know that they had an incredibly sophisticated form of architecture where they built walls out of stones[lxx,] using no cement yet they were crafted so perfectly that a razor blade would not fit in between the joints, and no one, to this day, seems to know how they did this. They were so knowledgeable in stonemasonry that the referred to the Spanish as the "Unskilled people", in Quechua of course.

It is also known that the Incas had an intricate knowledge of astronomy, and a highly developed agricultural system. They had a multifarious social strata and a system of taxation for which records had to be kept. They also had a complex network of cobbled roads and tracks which were used by runners known as Chatskis, who transferred documents in the form of a relay system. Each runner would run ten kilometres or so, between strategically positioned stations, to give a message to the next runner, who would run approximately ten kilometres to pass the message to the next runner who waited at the next station and so on. It is said that it was possible to deliver a message several thousand miles from the North of the Inca Empire in Colombia, to the South of the Empire in only a few days. If it were true that that the Inca had no written language exactly what form of information were they relaying? We've all played Chinese whispers, so we know how unreliable it would have been to pass messages by word of mouth only. There is no doubt that by the time the many reports arrived at their destinations they would have changed completely and this would undoubtedly have created some form of chaos in terms of communication.

It is therefore practically certain that, contrary to common European scholarly belief, that the Incas must have had some form of written word. After all the Inca Empire was a highly sophisticated, multifarious society. They had an incredible knowledge of the Universe, and were known to have had centres of learning. It seems utterly preposterous to suggest that the Incas did not have a written language; it quite simply doesn't make sense.

Furthermore I believe my suspicions are justified, not least because it is also well known that the Mayan libraries, that contained thousands upon thousands of papyrus documents, including detailed agricultural records, were destroyed by the Spanish

Conquistadores in Central America. These records were regarded as pagan literature, and were therefore extinguished in the name of Catholicism. It is also well known that the Maya travelled across the seas from Southern Mexico to trade with the Inca nations, which would imply that the known written language of the Maya[lxxi] would, at the very least, have transferred, to a certain degree, across cultures.

In fact I have been told in no uncertain terms by more than one local tourist guide in and around Cuzco that Inca documents are known to have been written in the form of Hieroglyphs and recognised, documented, examples of which were in existence long before the arrival of the Spaniards. I am confident that I would have been able to substantiate this, had the museum in Cuzco not have been closed each time I went to visit. It is also all too apparent that a great empire, such as that of the Spanish, would not now wish to admit to such unjustified destruction of the written word.

* * *

Marie Paz and I left Administrative Centre IV and walked up to the main part, or centre, of the city that had been cleared of jungle vegetation. This area was quite open, several of the larger more aristocratic houses adjacent to a large open lawn of possibly a hectare in size, from which can also be seen the remaining walls of a few smaller dwellings that were occupied by the lower echelons, had been cleared of the incumbency of undergrowth. From these houses a pathway can be taken up a hundred or so metres up to a small round plateau, about the size of a football pitch, that stands out, high above the Apurimac slopes, where all around is an incredible vista of the valleys below. This would surely have been used as a vantage point to warn of any unwanted visitors. From this outlook can also be seen the smaller dwellings of what could have been the priests' quarters situated up a small rise on the other side of the lawned green beneath, that looked down from the cliff edge onto the Apurimac valley below. This area is likely to be adjacent to a large number of small dwellings that are yet to be uncovered. Huge, five metre high grey stone terraces veer off to the side of the now lawned green, clearly they are only a few of a series of several more that step down the slope below, still covered by vegetation. There are many other buildings and terraces uncovered but clearly there are many more still obscured on a site that could be more than one hundred hectares in size.

The views from Choquekiraw are truly amazing; it is an incredible vantage point, high up in the Andes. Some say it was built as a military station, some say it was built after the Spanish conquest, as an escape from the tyranny, to retain La Nobleza; in effect a rebel city, I think not. I think it was built many, many, years before La Conquista, built as a place for the people to live closer to the Inca gods; a religious, spiritual place, where the people had chosen to live, well in advance of the advance of the Spanish. Yet nobody knows for certain when the city was built.

Choquekiraw had systems of showers and washrooms designed from a network of channels and a complex irrigation system to produce their plentiful crops on the terraces. They were able to live in harmony with nature in the mountains which they believed were great spirits, unlike in the western sense, where mountains are nothing more than great lumps of rock. Their Gods had given the Incas everything that they could have wished for, and for that they would have wished to give something in return. Choquekiraw is an incredibly beautiful, metaphysical, majestic and mysterious city.

* * *

As we walked across a wide open lawn Marie Paz and I got caught with no entrance tickets by one of the rangers, but she had no tickets either, so we promised to pay later on. As we walked back into the forest pathways towards the tourist centre, we got stung for Sol. 37 (£7.40) by another ranger along the way. They allowed me to pay for only one person because Marie Paz mentioned that she was a charity worker

205

in the community of Apuquri. So was I for that matter, but I, to them, was a wealthy foreigner, I was happy to pay.

After some confusion as to which pathway to take, we got back to the previous night's fire place atop the terraces; where we met our French drug smoking friend René at the uncannily deserted camp. It was a Godsend that he cooked up some more delicious chocolate soup and he also gave us some bread and cheese, which was only to be expected from a Frenchman. However, it came as somewhat of a surprise, and a certain disappointment, that he didn't manage to provide a 1964 Châteauneuf-du-Pape,[lxxii] or perhaps a Côte de Roussillon,[lxxiii] both of which are known to accompany cheese particularly well.

* * *

We should have stayed in Choquekiraw for another night, but sadly we had no food. I really have to return one day, maybe not today, maybe not tomorrow, but someday and someday soon. We departed at around 1.30 p.m. Much to my regret I left with some trepidation, I was still nervous of the height, but no doubt Marie Paz had no such concern about walking down slippery stone tracks, with certain death by her side. We could have so easily have found our final resting place on the journey down the mountainside, it was difficult to overcome my phobia.

We walked down along the pathways that sometimes tunnelled through the forest on the high slopes, then out into the open oblivion of the cliff side trails. The hike downward was clearly incredibly easy in comparison to the climb, in fact most of what I thought was unjustified apprehension had almost disappeared apart from where we came upon a few particularly sheer precipices. The descent became more like a rather rapid Sunday stroll than an exhausting hike. Marie Paz was moving as though she had taken some amphetamine of some kind; if she had some she certainly didn't offer me any. I found myself burdened with almost all of the equipment, including Dayme's blankets. I thought it was the gentlemanly thing to do.

The views on the way down were no less spectacular, and the loose stones made the pathway no less slippery underfoot, but we made good speed. After only an hour or so we could see the pattern of the fields that lay on the mountain slopes surrounding the old farm building far beneath us on the other side of the ravine. I had hardly before noticed the beautiful narrow waterfall that fell from hundreds of feet above it. It was easy to imagine how, in days gone by, probably over one hundred years beforehand, there had been a prosperous working farm below, busy with people and livestock.

There was little time for hesitation or rest and it was only 3.00 p.m. by the time we arrived at the river Apurimac, incredibly the descent had taken only one and a half hours. We crossed that bridge when we came to it and began the hike past La Playa up towards La Casa de San Ignacio. After such a rapid descent the walk back up to La Casa was considerably more difficult than I had anticipated. It took a two and half hours to hike up to La Casa, it wasn't until 5.30 that we finally arrived.

We were greeted by José when we got back to the very welcome Casa de San Ignacio, which was some relief. We sat exhausted at the table where we had eaten two nights before. We drank some of the local rum that José had bought for us along with some provisions the previous day from the local shop. The trek to the shop for José was no more than a stroll. He told us he could hike up an ascent of one kilometre in no more than a couple of hours and we believed him. On the day we had departed, he had climbed a few hundred metres up the mountain adjacent to the farm, and had descended to buy the goods from the shop in valley on the other side. He had then climbed back up the mountain from the shop and had returned to the lodge, and all before lunch. To have such flight of feet, was quite an incredible feat by anyone's standards.

Shortly after our arrival, while we were sat talking to José, we were joined briefly by a couple of teachers from Huanicapa, who were accompanied by a small group of noisy school children who strolled past us, in polite fashion, to the dormitories below. They were to stay at the Casa overnight en route to Choquekiraw. The youngsters were very cheerful when they waved as they passed us on the way down to the lodge directly beneath us. The teachers were very polite when they paused only to talk to us briefly. They were quite inquisitive as to where we were from, though were not particularly forthcoming themselves I didn't find them to be quite as simpático as the Apuqurians that I knew, in any way at all.

As night fell, Marie Paz cooked us some soup from the remnants of the tuna and onion, along with some papas, which was most welcome. The soup was followed by plentiful bowls of mango and papaya, accompanied by some orange juice and a little rum of course, but sadly no bears.

We were in bed by 9.00 p.m. in the stone cold, vacuous rooms of the lodge, separately, as you would expect. I slept like a baby.

Thursday 24ᵗʰ September

Marie Paz and I were up at 5.00 a.m., I had a freezing shower. Marie Paz made a breakfast of bread, tomato and onion salsa on an open fire, a considerably warmer occupation. I paid José a few Sol. which we had agreed for the food that he had provided for us, plus a little extra.

We set off at 8.20 a.m. precisely; the rucksack was now repacked and was heavy laden with Dayme's blankets and the Italian tent. The hike up the gentle undulating slope of the vale that led from La Casa de San Ignacio was again far more demanding than anticipated. In the heat of the day, we stopped at a brook, by the sun drenched pathway. We washed in the cool, fresh, clear water and filled a couple of bottles from the stream that fell towards the gorge beneath us.

It was a long hard, uneventful hike back up the tributary valley beneath the bright sunlight. The slope on the way down had seemed slight, but the return journey was a different matter altogether. It was the same beautiful place but the burden of my rucksack was weighing heavy upon my shoulders. Marie Paz, I have to say had incredible stamina; she didn't seem to tire at all.

It wasn't until 1.30 p.m. that we arrived at the Hotel de Los Lorros, it had been a five hour hike and we were thoroughly exhausted. When we got there we were greeted by the Italian lady who was far more amenable on this occasion. She readily called us our taxi driving friend and we paid her Sol. 29, which was calculated as Sol. 15, or half price for the use of the tent, which we didn't use, plus the phone calls and some coffee, fair enough I thought.

Despite several promises the taxi didn't arrive until it was getting dark early that evening. This meant that we were left with nothing to do all afternoon which did become tiresome as we both wanted to be on our way.

We spent the afternoon in the well-kept garden. For the sake of amusement, I showed Marie Paz some Aikido Ukemi, or how to fall over in Japanese. We had Tiffin at four, with some super cucumber triangles and a spot of carrot cake. We spoke to the Italian lady about the possibility of sending people over from the UK to stay in the hotel en route to Choquekiraw. We talked about other things, such as the Inca society, and I remember when talking, that she was incredibly certain of her Peruvian history and I also remember being incredibly certain that I didn't agree with her, in a polite way of course. She also told us how she had her coffee sent over from Italy, which was interesting considering most of the coffee in the world is produced in South America, so by the time she drank it, it was quite well travelled. I think she may have softened by the time we left that evening.

After quite a long afternoon, our amenable young friend arrived in his silver Japanese estate car. As luck would have it, he offered to take us all the way to Abancay via Huanicapa for Sol. 80 (£16.00), which was a far better prospect than going back to spend another night in the village and then to descend the following day, after searching for another taxi. It took us until shortly before 8.00 p.m. to get back to Huanicapa, where we stopped at a shop on the plaza, where our driver told his parents that he was taking us to Abancay. It also gave him the chance to collect his mate who sat in the front beside him. We bought some sweets and bread from his family's arcadian store, and I had the chance to use the convenience that was a small brick shed out in the back garden. This time around the people in the store seemed far more open and friendly than before, though that may have been because we were employing their son.

The night was dark, damp and miserable, a mist had fallen all around us when we left Huanicapa, and visibility was low. There are no street lights in the mountains and the track that our driver took us on for over an hour was quite rough, but this didn't perturb him one little bit. As he drove he seemed to be getting more and more confident, as his confidence increased so did his speed in a Peruvian style that I had seen several times before. This time we were going around bends on a gravel track, enveloped by clouds, on a murky night, where a small mistake could mean certain death, it was getting just a little too dangerous. I waited for some time, but I had no choice, I could wait no longer, I threw any machismo I may have had out the window, I had to ask our budding Sebastian Loeb to slow down; which thankfully he did, as there aren't too many Peruvian Rally champions. The main reason presumably being because one slip on those mountain roads doesn't mean a few small scratches and the occasional dent, it means sayonara, or goodnight Vienna.

When we pulled off the mountain track we drove out onto the luxury of a broad, modern, sweeping metalled road that passed down from the elevation of the mountains into Abancay an hour or so below. We were stopped on the way down at a road block by some armed police waving luminous green battens, who wanted to check our documents.

Although seemingly officious, this fortunately brief respite turned out to be nothing more than routine.

After our long mountainous descent we drove through the unkempt outskirts of Abancay, where the air was clear dry and warm, the climate had changed to that of a pleasant summer's evening. Thereafter our driver kindly took us into the centre of town, to a street where he told us knew we would find a good inexpensive hotel. He was right, behind an iron barred door we found a really good cheap scruffy hotel that we entered through a narrow corridor that would hardly be noticed from the street. My room was quite small and was slightly unkempt, but there was electric light, there was hot water, it was warm, there was a TV protruding from the wall high above the end of the bed, with more than two channels, to me this modest room was absolute luxury.

I soaked up the relative luxury of the modern convenience of a downtown Peruvian Hotel for as long as I could. I could actually flip though more than two channels, whilst I lay on the bed watching TV. I took a warm en suite shower, something I hadn't done for quite some time and then, when I had freshened up I went out to find Marie Paz. She was in a room along one of the narrow corridors nearby.

We walked out of the hotel into the busy streets of Abancay, in search of some traditional Peruvian food, which after some exploration we could not find. So we settled for some traditional fried chicken and chips, from another sparse menu in a well presented, local restaurant which was almost hidden down one of the side streets. It had a clement, accommodating atmosphere and the food was, in fact, very good. It is almost impossible to buy chicken in Peru which is anything other than organic, and it tastes completely different to deep fried pre-processed battery hen.

When we had left the restaurant we found a lot of people walking through the dusky streets, there was something afoot that night. We found that there were many people congregating in a square close by, a salsa band with guitars and a brass section, that was about to play on an elevated stage on one side of the plaza. At the front of the band there was a line of smartly dressed men in suits, taking turns to sing, whilst dancing to the vibrant salsa beat of a pair of drummers in the background, accompanied by a few pretty girls who sang and danced the accompaniment, all in animated, perfect rhythmic time. It was a spectacular show, the Salsa Brothers had come to town and the whole place was dancing. Marie Paz showed me a few Latin steps, which were not so easy, but I managed reasonably well and we danced the night away.

After some time, a wooden framed tower and some other effigies of wood and paper were brought into the far side of the square, which some officials proceeded to burn in the street adjacent to the crowd, whilst they also set off some fireworks. Some might say that this was a little risqué and others would say it was positively dangerous, I didn't find it to be so.

We discovered that the spectacle was all in celebration of the beginning of the new semester at the University of Abancay. It was a fantastic evening, the atmosphere was incredible and we couldn't have planned it better. We both thoroughly enjoyed our brief excursion, we had arrived by coincidence on exactly the right day.

As the crowd subsided we walked back to the hotel quite late at around 1.00 a.m. Back in my room I couldn't resist watching the North American film "Road Trip, The Movie" in English, until the early hours. Not my normal choice but I

213

hadn't seen a full length movie, or anything else for that matter, in English, for almost a month. I slept very well that night.

Friday 25th September

I awoke at 7.30 a.m., showered, got dressed and went to collect Marie Paz from her room; she was already up and packed.

Marie Paz and I paid our bill and left our bags at the hotel; then we walked out into the bustling streets, past the many shops that splayed out onto the pavements. After a short while we arrived at a large covered market where the campesinos were selling their wares on the sides of the road adjacent. The place was alive with energy; the people were all really friendly and cheerful. We sat at one of the many breakfast bars in the busy market where most of the menus were basically the same, which meant that there wasn't much choice; the young woman dished out rice, potatoes, chicken and pork all covered in a creamy sauce, I was told that this was known as Raduche. It was incredibly fresh, organic, delicious and very nourishing.

The market traders were laughing and joking as we passed by the stalls. Marie Paz stocked up on provisions, for life back in Apuquri, such as pulses, various vegetables and some lamb, which I paid for of course. It was ironic that whilst we were in mid-market mode, out of the blue my girlfriend called me from England on my mobile, at a particularly inopportune moment; which was whilst I was walking through the large open indoor market, amidst cat calls from some of the ladies who ran the stalls. They asked me if I had a girlfriend, which I did, I said, "Actually she's on the phone now", but that didn't perturb them. I spoke only very briefly to my girlfriend, it was just a little awkward, and quite noisy, but I did say "Of course I do", miss her that is. I may have forgotten to mention that most of the stall holders seemed to have a girlfriend whom they wanted to introduce me to. I got a few marriage proposals that morning, they were all joking of course, which was all very funny, it was a beautiful uplifting day in Abancay.

My girlfriend and I hardly ever spoke whilst I was in South America, the cost was prohibitive. I was almost always out of signal, emails are not always the best way to communicate I have found, and there was no Skype at the time. She wasn't happy that I was away. I wasn't happy that she wasn't happy at me being away either. In fact I wanted her to come and join me later on, when I had left the mountains; but she wouldn't accept me spending time in South America, even though I had my reasons. I wasn't being wayward, I did nothing that I shouldn't have, but she was using female logic again, which left me somewhat confused.

On the way out from the market, by some coincidence, we met Juan Carlos who told us he was in Abancay buying materials for the job. He was looking for the best deal he could find on the Teja Andina, the terracotta roof tile, which did have its demands. Juan Carlos needed to find the right quality tiles at the right price and he also had to negotiate a fair price for the transport of the tiles to Apuquri. He was his usual jovial self, but there were always mixed emotions when we saw him. He was a very likeable guy, but he was never entirely straight with us, there was always something hidden. We only spoke for a short while and then we went our separate ways.

I needed a haircut so Marie Paz and I walked through some of the side streets in search of a hairdresser for me. What was strange was that Marie Paz had someone in mind, but she didn't say a word to me about that. This meant that we looked at a couple of barbers and then we just somehow arrived at a hairdresser that seemed to be the right one, and she happened to be the friend of Marie Paz's that I realised she had had in mind all along.

She was in her thirties and quite glamorous, in fact very attractive. She was incredibly well groomed as are most female hairdressers. She moved in a very slow precise way and took great care in what she did. I remember that she sent a shiver down my spine when she cut my hair, especially when she blew on the back of my neck. Of all the haircuts in all of the world, that is the one I will remember before all others. I have never experienced anything like it before or since, which I suppose may be because I generally cut my own hair. However her effect on me was undeniably extraordinary.

With my brand new haircut, I felt quite refreshed and glad that I hadn't drunk any chicha beforehand. We walked up into the centre of town where we came upon a food fair along a main thoroughfare, which was not entirely unlike a Peruvian Style farmers' market. There were various food stands selling local produce, people were selling honey, many different cheeses, many types of bread, organically grown beef, chicken, pork, lamb and llama; which is in fact delicious. Unfortunately there were no examples of guinea pigs, which are regarded as something of a delicacy in Peru. All of the food on sale was in the main organic by circumstance and relatively free of any unnatural western additives, a quality quite noticeable in comparison to the food sold in the over processed supermarkets of much of Europe and North America.

Abancay was moving trade into the modern way. There was salsa playing around the various stalls and the place was bustling with people. There were also a few glamorous young women providing a cocktail making display. It was interesting and highly entertaining, in particular to see cocktail shakers thrown about the place. I was expecting Tom Cruise to arrive at any moment.

As we walked down the street in the centre of town, Marie Paz and I found ourselves a sparse clean Chinese restaurant with photos on the menu, because that was where we could find her favourite food. We both had a delicious Wanton soup for lunch, which was incredibly nutritious and incredibly cheap. It only cost about Sol. 10 or two quid for two. I really must learn how to make that, that is definitely on the list.

At around 5.00 p.m. we took a colectivo[lxxiv] that we had found in town after some enquiry, which took us back on a comfortable ride, on the well-made road, through the spectacular scenery of the Andes to Chalhuanca.

During the journey Marie Paz told me of the way of the campesinos. She told me of the peace that the country people seek, how they wish to live in harmony with mother nature and do not wish for the confrontation as the first world seems to perceive. They are a warm gentle people who do not live by any false, shallow, desires of materialism, which can be said is the infestation of the world of consumerism. I believe the principle is referred to as "fatsheed" or something similar. If one is to understand these principles then a visit to these remote areas becomes far more rewarding; especially if the xenophobia inbred within us is considered and brushed aside. When I was in Peru, at the risk of being melodramatic, I found that if you love the people around you, they will love you back; including the minors in theory, but that is unlikely. There is a lot of love in the mountains.

When we arrived in the darkness of the early evening at around 7.00 p.m, we found a standard dark blue Japanese estate car fairly easily; it took us back up to Apuquri without much delay. The driver stopped on the way to fill up and collect his wife, which seemed to be normal for taxi drivers on frequent occasion. The ride was fairly dangerous, the driver seemed to be in a hurry, which as normal, while driving up a cliff side track, did not create a peaceful easy feeling. Nonetheless, I decided to keep my mouth shut, I thought that my trepidation was probably only that of the still unaccustomed tourist. I also noticed that the miners had begun upgrading the road at the base of the track and I wondered if they had permission, it seemed that they were a law unto themselves.

The lights of Apuquri were a welcome sight when they glistened before us through the darkness on the final bend at around 9.30 p.m. It was cold that night but it was good to be back at my by now familiar home from home, that had no heating, virtually no TV, and an earthen floor. The guinea pigs, the various dogs, cows and chickens that we lived beside were good company. We didn't eat that evening because Juan Carlos still had the gas ring burners; he clearly hadn't thought that we might need them. The house was far from luxurious by first world standards but it was the soul and serenity of the place that filled me with the comfortable warmth of home.

Before we retired we shared a couple of glasses of rum to warm us up whilst watching one of the two TV channels, through the misty vapour of our breath, before we went to bed, separately of course. I slept very well that freezing cold night under my twelve blankets, with my Deet on my hands.

Saturday 26th September

I awoke at 7.30 a.m. I had sunshine on a cloudy day, it was cold outside, but it was a beautiful day. I had my usual Englishman's wash and a rather indulgent breakfast, and the dogs returned to say hello, I was pleased to get back to work, albeit late at 10.00 a.m.

When we got to the site we discovered that the Tejas Andinas[lxxv] had been delivered, Juan Carlos later told me the cost, a huge amount of money for Peru:

Sol. 500 per 1000 = Sol. 4,000 + transport Sol. 2,000 = Sol. 6,000 (£1200)

Apparently during the past week Juan Carlos had been in Cuzco Monday and Tuesday arranging the buying of the roof tiles, Wednesday and Thursday they said he was helping on the site from 8.00 a.m. until 5.00 p.m. (I didn't believe that for a moment). The day before he had been in Abancay for the morning, he came back and then disappeared again at 2.00 p.m., he was due to return from Abancay on Monday next.

I could see no reason why Juan Carlos should have had to return to Abancay other than by reason of a local Doris, but that was his business. However his absence did leave us with a minor problem; we could not cook on the gas rings, they were locked in the municipal buildings and Juan Carlos would do as he pleased, and we knew of no one else who had any keys.

It was a great day at work, Andino and another, who I did not know, were bringing the adobe bricks in wheel barrows down the slope from where they had been drying. I was placing them neatly in stacks close to the ends of the building in preparation for the construction of the eaves, where they would be cut and used to fill in between the roof joists. I really enjoyed working as a hod carrier there; we were making jokes all day, working out in the clean fresh air, beneath the sunshine.

In view of the fact that the gas hobs were locked away, certain expletives sprung to mind as me and Hercules walked up the declivitous pathway together carrying leña[lxxvi] that we had collected and wrapped in a blue blanket that we hung over our shoulders in turn. It was hard work, walking up that precipice in the thin air of the Andes.

We walked past our brown eyed friends that I had met on the first day, they were sitting on the grey stone walls of a small paddock, attempting to catch two large, impressively horned Toros Bravos.[lxxvii] They were to harness them in a yoke so that they could be taken up the cákras for ploughing, and they were clearly enjoying themselves. It was a fairly dangerous pastime, dodging the sharp horns of the bulls, but a lot easier after a few drinks. There was an old lady dressed in many skirts and fedora in attendance to maintain high spirits in the form of the local whisky. She gave both me and Hercules a glass and then another, it would have been rude not to partake, whilst we chatted to the men.

Following a couple of shots of rum, we walked up the hill, Hercules departed and I took the wood in so that Marie Paz could cook us some lunch. Marie Paz did not complain once that she had no gas hobs to cook on, not once.

After lunch we carried on shifting the adobe bricks into stacks for the gables at either end of the building, we did a very neat professional job, under my guidance, I might add.

The two lads did a great job with the heavy wheelbarrows, while I was stacking and loading out. It was a very fulfilling workout, and much better than being in the gym. I was a hod carrier once more, albeit at 3,700 metres above sea level. I was balancing along the walls carrying heavy adobe bricks to Fernando and Roger; as I may have mentioned, I was quite content, and happy in that work.

As the day drew to an end, I sent one of the lads up to buy cañazo and coke, which we mixed with a little water in a large coke bottle. The team were all very appreciative of a drink at the end of the day. I was honoured to be invited by Edwin, who had turned up out of the blue, to help in La Sembra[lxxviii] in the cákra just above Marie Paz's house, at the end of the street. Of course I accepted his kind offer but sadly it never came to fruition, and it wasn't a Californian invitation, it was just that I was too committed to the building of the Casa Hogar,[lxxix] which may have been a mistake in retrospect, because I would have liked to spend some time working in the cákras.

At the end of the day I asked the workers if anyone had a hammer; we were just about to start the tiling of the roof, so we would need a few hammers. "Has anyone got a hammer," they looked at each other, "Don Antonio, you've got a hammer haven't you?" they said, "Yes I think I've got a hammer" "Well can you bring it in Monday?" I said. "I will if I can find it, I haven't seen it for a while, I might have lent it to my cousin" said Don Antonio. So I asked if anyone else had a hammer, they looked at me and said no they didn't. I said, "So nobody has a hammer except Don Antonio, who may or may not be able to find the one he has". "Yes" they said, that is apart from Don Moreno, he had a hammer, but he wasn't going to be working on the tiling of the roof. They said one hammer should be enough. I said no way, we had a lot of battens to nail in place, so I would go down to Chalhuanca the next day and buy some, hammers that is.

After we had cleared up me and Hercules gathered a little more wood to again carry home in the blue blanket, across our shoulders as before, so that Marie Paz had something to cook with. We shared the burden on the way back to the house; it didn't get any lighter, to say the least.

After supper that evening I asked why the dogs were making so much noise, they seemed a little crazy; the noise was rising to a loud crescendo. Marie Paz told me that was because of the new moon, of course, how stupid of me not to have realised.

It was cold, but I slept very well that night under my twelve blankets, despite the noise of the dogs; they did eventually calm down.

Sunday 27th September

I got up at 8.00 a.m., washed and had another breakfast of fresh organic eggs, I imagine it is easy to see that I was well catered for. Life was a pleasure in the mountains of Apuquri, far from the stresses and strains of modern civilisation. Though it was cold at night, the sun shone every day, the air, although admittedly very thin, was crisp, clean and fresh, the birds were singing and today I was going to have a bath.

Marie Paz and I walked down into the centre of the village, where we easily found a taxi into Chalhuanca. When we arrived we went into the uneventful internet café for a short while. I didn't want to spend time in front of a computer if I could avoid it, especially when I could be walking in the mountains. I remember I still had a few seemingly irrelevant problems with the University that I had to resolve, and someone had sent me a link, which was nice.

The problem I had was that I had been trying to get some information that I needed from the information department at the University and they told me that I was looking for the wrong kind of information as the information I wanted was not the information that was part of their remit and so they very kindly sent me a link. When I clicked on that link and made a further inquiry, and they very kindly, sent me to another link, which sent me to another link, and then another link and another. Finally, when a few months had passed, I got back to the original link. It must be because people now have jobs sending links to people because nobody actually wants to do anything. I believe mainly for two reasons, one they can't be bothered to help anyone anymore and two, because if they actually did something then they could possibly get blamed if it went wrong, so therefore it is better not to do anything except send a link. In consequence there are whole office departments that are dedicated to sending links, where the staff are trained how to do avoid doing anything else. Sadly when people do nothing for years, they lose the ability to actually do anything at all, because eventually they forget how to do anything, and then what do they tell their Grandchildren?

I had no real problems with links in Peru, apart from the link to the miners and underlying threat of annihilation of course, but I had long since put that to one side, after all, that was only a matter of life and death.

* * *

When I had managed to escape from the internet café we found a taxi, in the form of yet another dark blue Japanese estate car, that took us across the river Apurimac behind the main town centre, up along a glorious dusty, earthen, tree lined track into the open cliff side roads up to the Baños Termales de Pincahuacho[lxxx] that rested on the side of a mountain slope adjacent to a few rustic dwellings, at 3100 metres above sea level, a few miles out of town. There we came upon a large whitewashed building, above a 25 meter swimming pool at the bottom of a grass slope beneath, that presented a row of green wooden doors which opened into incredibly large individual pristine, white tiled bathrooms. I paid my dues, took the keys, gave Marie Paz hers, and we agreed to meet an hour later, which could have only been a guess as I had no watch, and neither did Marie Paz. I went to open my private bathroom door and filled a large white ceramic tiled rectangular bath with hot spring water from the enormous brass taps. I undressed and proceeded to have my first bath since England. The water, slightly murky, was very warm and incredibly pleasant, all very Romanesque and incredibly satisfying.

When our time was up, after the awarded hour or so, Marie Paz and I met outside and walked up to our awaiting taxi, which had acquired a few more passengers. We drove down the cliff side road towards Chalhuanca, which were quite unnerving because they were so open and exposed, the incline over the edge was undoubtedly a matter of certain death, but as usual, to the local people it was nothing out of the ordinary, while I was sitting in the passenger seat trying to press imaginary brake pedals. When we stopped to pass an oncoming car, the driver would edge to within an inch of the cliff edge, and stop and have a chat with the other driver, and no one gave a damn, except for me of course. Nonetheless the view was spectacular whereby we could see all away down the valley where the streets of Chalhuanca rested below. I just didn't want to fall into it, which I didn't think was not entirely unreasonable.

When we arrived in Chalhuanca we went directly to the hardware store with our shopping list where I bought four candles, three hammers, two with bright orange handles and one bright yellow, and a few kilos of nails as ordered for the roof battens. Total cost Sol. 178 including Sol. 60 for the taxi. It didn't make me unhappy to buy the hardware but the principle didn't make me too happy to be doing a job that Juan Carlos was getting paid for.

It was going to be time for me to leave in a few days, so when we had bought a few provisions we went to a bus agency, and booked a seat for me to take a return bus ride for Lima, for Friday next at 7.00 p.m. We didn't buy the cheapest ticket; Marie Paz reinforced the fact that a bus ride in Peru is not always the safest form of transport.

When we had procured my ticket, as was normal we spent some time looking for a taxi to take us back up to Apuquri, which became an uneventful, musical cliff side drive, that we shared with a couple of the locals from the village.

That night Marie Paz and I talked about how the miners had begun the construction of the infrastructure to mine gold; even though they had no right to start work without a contractual agreement to do so. It seemed that they did as they pleased, that may have been because they quite simply had too much power.

Marie Paz was educated and certainly politically aware, she was also considered to be a pillar of the community. Marie Paz said that she considering becoming a member of the local council, from where she could block the proposed mining project, which could have created some unrest and that was a dangerous position to be in. It became increasingly apparent that the power of political economics would take precedence over the welfare of the people. The governing bodies of the community did not want to see change. There is more than enough potential profit available from the extraction of minerals in South America to reduce the problems of illiteracy and develop the agricultural infrastructure, as there used to be before Spanish imperialism, but sadly the western banks want to maintain the status quo as it stands, in order to retain their power base. Therein lies the dichotomy, an influx of money would destroy the tranquillity of mountain life, as it is today, where the people are in the most part content and accept what would seem to be a hardship of subsistence in the developed world. Though better schools and healthcare would certainly be beneficial and also some assistance in the reconstitution of the agricultural infrastructure as it was before the Spanish invasion.

This destruction of the environment is totally unnecessary, not only is there enough underdeveloped land to feed the indigenous population, but they could also produce sufficient volume of crops for export. There is no need to destroy rainforest or any other areas for a fast buck, to do so is utter madness and those that do so should be taken to task, naming no names, Monsanto, for example.

The problem is so bad that those who attempt to interfere and actually improve the situation have a tendency to disappear, but sadly the irony exists that if we continue on this road, we could all disappear. There is no logic that I am aware of that would suggest otherwise. It seems that the world has gone crazy in the short term pursuit of the satisfaction of greed, but none of us have time to think about that, because we are all too busy paying our bills.

The situation is such that those in power want to maintain the current political situation to such an extent that Marie Paz, if she were able to, as an elected member of office, would be in a position where her life would be under threat. She actually told me that she was prepared to stand up and speak for the campesinos, even if that put her life at in danger, but sadly that may be too high a mountain for her to climb, and she already lives at 3700m above sea level.

* * *

We also talked about how in the early eighteen hundreds the Spanish had built a small hamlet, from where the people panned for gold. It was situated by a river in a valley on the high plains, situated way up behind Apu San Francisco, but had long since been abandoned. It consisted of a handful of small straw roofed, grey stone houses built adjacent to a church. Apparently a few years beforehand, it was rumoured that one of the communities nearby, where the character of the people is not quite as genteel as that of the people of Apuquri, were going to move in and take possession of the area. In consequence many of the men, women and children of Apuquri went up the mountain at the time of the proposed invasion and slept there the night, or several nights, in order to maintain their claim over the land. Which, as it has turned out, was a wise move, because that is the same area from which the miners were intending to extract the gold.

* * *

That night the dogs were getting quite loud as the full moon was approaching, it was due on Thursday. Marie Paz told me la sembra would be two days afterwards. In order to attain the most abundant crop, the seeds would be sewn in the cákras two days after the full moon, when the moon had just begun to wane.

I drank a little too much cañazo that evening before I went to bed, but it did help me get to sleep eventually that freezing night, to the sound of the dogs barking, at what seemed to be at not too great a distance. They were getting really noisy; the effect of the full moon was really quite astounding.

Monday 28th September

We had breakfast at around 8.00 a.m., but nothing of note really happened. We were down on the site at 9.00 a.m. when we began moving the roof battens close to the walls of the building, in preparation for the construction of the roof. These bunches of battens were really heavy, and the men, though somewhat condensed in the height department, were able to carry them without much difficulty. However for my part I had to get used to the weight.

When we had moved a few bundles we climbed up onto the walls where the trusses had been put in place using random battens to hold them in position, much in the same manner as would be done on any building site in England. I gave the men the brightly handled hammers, and I was actually quite taken aback at their criticism of the quality of the tools that I had bought. The hammers were given a miserable reception but the men seemed nonetheless pleased, and were quite happy to make use of them. They began cutting the battens in preparation and nailing some in situ.

I continued carrying the battens down the slope until we all stopped for lunch at 12 noon, when, I, of course, walked back up to Marie Paz's with Hercules as usual, where she had made a soup full of lamb stock and herbs, rice, and papas, which I followed with a brief, but much needed, afternoon nap.

I got back down to work at 1.45 p.m. and moved some more bundles of battens down ready to be measured and cut for the roof. I climbed up onto the walls and noticed that one man was banging a nail in, and five were watching, which was painfully slow and frustrating to watch. So I looked at them and asked why they didn't work in three teams of two as what they were doing was incredibly lackadaisical, or the Spanish equivalent. They weren't too pleased at this suggestion and they didn't seem altogether bothered by the speed of the construction. I am certain this was because they were getting paid by the day, and the longer the job took the more money they made, not least because employment was not exactly prevalent in the area, apart from that which could be found in the cákras, which was, almost always, unpaid. I didn't manage to succeed in organising three teams of two, but I did manage two teams of three, which was not the easiest of tasks. At the end of the day we had only completed three sections with roof battens, which was rather slower than I would have hoped, and not really my responsibility, but I did my best. Nonetheless the men made me feel a lot like an outsider that day.

All was not lost though, four unattended bulls wandered through the site while we were working which was a joy and there was no sign of Juan Carlos. We finished at the normal time and I walked back up to Marie Paz's with Hercules, where we said farewell for the day.

Marie Paz and I were going to buy a beer from the shop opposite the front of the house, when we met a woman in the street. The woman was carrying a bucket, and the bucket was filled with small trout that had been caught in the lake high up above, on the other side of somewhere. They were of course fresh so we bought thirteen for the princely sum of Sol. 3 which at the time was about 60p. So to add the luxury of fresh trout for supper I bought a bottle of what turned out to be a very sweet red wine that came from the desert town of Ica, at a cost from the store of Sol. 2.50 or 50p.

We then went on our way to the end of the road to find a taxi driver, who we hoped would take us into Chalhaunca to buy baby chickens the following day, which I wanted to give to Cleo Fé, as gift. I thought she might like to have a few more eggs. I don't know why we needed to arrange a special taxi. I would have thought that chicken transit is a speciality of all forms of transport in South America. Nonetheless we had little luck, we couldn't find the taxi driver, but we did find a fridge at Marie Paz's friend's house where we could store some of the trout for another day.

On the way we found some muña, a herb that we picked to make an anti-mosquito lotion with water, which apparently is also good for rheumatism. Another herb another day, yet it was incredible how the knowledge of the people of the mountains could benefit medicine throughout the world, and it's only been tested for 7,000 years.

When we got back home, we had some soup and a couple of drinks. We watched "The last of the Samurai" with Tom Cruise, well perhaps not with him; he was in the film on TV. We then, quite tired, retired to bed in the cold as I was accustomed to do, well almost.

* * *

When I was in Lima a few weeks later, on a bus on the way back from a day out at the zoo in Lima, with the kids from the orphanage, I told the women carers how we had bought the Trucha, (or trout) from the woman I the street in Apuquri. With big smiles on their faces they asked me if I liked Trucha, did I like the taste, was it my favourite? Did I like Trucha a lot? And they began laughing when I said, "Yes I did, in fact, it is my favourite." They asked me about the Trucha for quite some time and began laughing in hysterics, when eventually I caught on that something was wrong. I soon realised that Trucha, in Liman slang, has another meaning apart from trout. These seemingly conservative women of the orphanage managed to keep that joke going until the time I left the place, more than two weeks later. They would say things like, "Would you like Trucha today?"

"Is it your favourite?"

"Do you like the taste?"

"You must be pleased; we have Trucha again for lunch today."

Tuesday 29th September

I got up, and had a wash as normal in the chill of the bright sunshine, while Marie Paz prepared breakfast. I said good morning to the dogs and greeted a family as they herded their flock of sheep along the street in front of the house. Cleo Fé chased one of her cows out of her kitchen in reverse and I managed to eject a chicken from the living room, a normal morning in fact.

We walked down to work with the dogs at around 9.00 a.m. The men were listless, they were about to mark out to cut and place the battens. I think Marie Paz must have had a quiet word, they continued to work in two teams of three. I set to work cutting battens marked by the men in advance, to speed the job up in a form of specialized methodology. This was much more efficient than before, which I was pleased to see, it enabled us to complete seven sections that day.

Juan Carlos turned up at around midday and had a bit of a chat, but he did no work at all. He joined me at Marie Paz's for lunch at around 12.30 p.m. and came back to the site for a short while afterwards, but he did not lift a finger. He returned late in the day and he came back up to Marie Paz's for dinner with me after work, via the off licence, where we bought some cañazo in preparation for the evening.

Marie Paz cooked us some very healthy broth with potatoes and rice, then she went to bed early at 9.30 p.m. shortly after we had eaten, I don't know why she left so early. Juan Carlos stayed up with me for a while and we drunk the cañazo, which was quite strong. He also ate some avocado and bread we had, colloquially known as "Bocadillo de Palta"[lxxxi] I don't remember why, but I ate nothing, which was probably a mistake.

Whilst we were talking, after a few sherbets, Juan Carlos told me, in no uncertain terms, that the community had signed the contract which had relinquished their rights over the extraction of the gold; in effect for a couple of computers and a tractor. I found this information very disturbing, but said little about it.

Juan Carlos seemed fine when he staggered home at around midnight. When I went to bed I was a little worse for wear, perhaps I should have had a palta sandwich.

* * *

There was a woman from Peru who I shared a kitchen with for a short time at University. To show some hospitality, when we first met I said to her, "Look if you run out of food, feel free to take some of mine, but please replace anything you take, and please leave me enough bread for toast in the morning" She said, "That's very kind, if you want to borrow any of mine please do the same, take it from my cupboard that is here." The next morning I walked into the kitchen and opened my cupboard, there was no bread. I scratched my head and wondered where a whole new sliced wholemeal loaf had suddenly disappeared to. At that moment the same Peruvian woman walked into the kitchen, and after I had told her of my problem she said, "Don't worry take some of mine" and handed me my loaf that she had taken from my cupboard without having said a word. How strange people can be.

Wednesday 30th September

I woke around eight and had a normal morning, nothing unusual about my wash, nothing unusual at breakfast, nothing unusual about various animals being chased around the garden by an 84 year old woman, nothing unusual on the way to work at around 9.00 a.m. with Marie Paz and the dogs. At least, that is, in the Apuqurian sense.

Once again I set to building the roof, with the men, nailing the battens in place. They marked the position of the battens, measured and marked the length, then passed them to me to cut; which I did for both teams of three. I passed them back, and they nailed them in place. This system was quite efficient, much quicker than before and the men were pleased.

The Alcalde, El Presidente and the Assistant El Presidente arrived mid-morning, seemingly from nowhere, in a silver 4 x 4 and greeted us all in a very jovial manner. All three of them were in a good mood and I doubt the driver would have passed a breathalyser. They then climbed onto the back of the pick-up truck, and promptly threw two dead pigs off the back; the pigs had blood markings from shotgun wounds in their black hair. Marie Paz arrived at more or less the same time, and told me that the Counsellors had been high up in the hills above Apuqri where pigs could be found that ran wild. A few pigs had been released up there years beforehand and had bred. The custom was for us to celebrate the gift of the pigs with a few beers, so I went up and bought a case of 12 beers at a cost of Sol. 30 which was not very much at all.

Don Moreno made a fire with Oscar under an open ended oil drum that had been filled with water; it had also appeared from seemingly nowhere. They needed to heat the water apparently, and proceeded to dunk the pigs and scrape the hair from the carcasses.

This was a good excuse for us all to stop work to have a drink and it seemed to me that the officials were only really topping themselves up. A friend of Marie Paz's, Micarella Bastida, a woman who was a school teacher, arrived from, again, seemingly nowhere, and had a drink with us. She was also a historian of some kind and took some pleasure in telling me of the division of the Inca Empire, when the brothers Huasca and Atahualpa had fought for power in 1532, and how Huasca had been killed by his brother. She also told me of the story of how Atahualpa was captured at Cajamarca, how the Inca gold had been taken and how Atahualpa was murdered by the Spanish, contrary to their promise.

Then she told me how the Spanish had murdered again when they killed the last of the Incas, Tupac Amaru, in 1572. Accused of leading a rebellion, the Spanish had pursued him and taken him to be executed in the central plaza of Cuzco. She told me that he was hung drawn and quartered after having witnessed the execution of most of the members of his family.

This may not have been entirely true as some reports say that he was beheaded. Other witnesses reported that as he mounted the black draped scaffolding built for his execution, between 10 and 15,000 people were present and that "a multitude of Indians, who completely filled the square, saw that lamentable spectacle and knew that their Lord and Inca was about to die. They deafened the skies, making them reverberate with their cries and wailing", as reported by Baltasar de Ocampa and Friar Gabriel de Oviedo, prior of the Dominicans of Cuzco. The Sapa Inca, raised his hand to silence the crowds and his last words were:

"Collanan pachacamac ricuy aucacunac yahuarniy hichascancuta" or "Mother earth, witness how my enemies shed blood".

This execution was not approved of by King Philippe II of Spain. This was because, by executing a head of state recognised by the Spanish as an independent King, the Viceroy of Toledo was exceeding his authority and had committed a crime contrary to the political laws of the time.

Cuzco being only around 110 miles from Apuquri, as the crow flies,[lxxxii] admittedly over one of the most mountainous regions in the world, was not too far away.

* * *

I watched the men sear the pigs when the water boiled, and when they scraped the hair off the bodies by the side of the site. This was not a pretty sight either, especially when they took all the guts out, which were carried up to the top of town much later, for the Pumas and Condors or whatever other scavenger may arrive.

I was disappointed to see that the Peruvians do not know how to perform a matanza[lxxxiii] as the Spanish do, where every single part of the animal is used, nothing is wasted. For example the offal and the blood are used to make sausages such as chorizo or morcilla (blood sausage). The people of the mountains are not wealthy, and the meat, and in

239

particular the offal, that they discard quite simply goes to the dogs. Peruvian food is good, there are many wonderful dishes that emanate from the country but it seems to me that the Peruvian culture would seriously benefit from a visit from a senior sausage manufacturer, like Walls; there are other manufacturers.

When the carcasses had been gutted and cleaned I helped carry them down in a wheel barrow, to a friend's house just down the slope around the corner from the site. It was dark and getting cold by the time we had hung the carcasses and finished tidying up at around 7.00 p.m.; so naturally we went to Roger's for a few beers.

That evening I proposed that we spit roast the pigs, to which they all agreed and then they again proposed that I be Padrino of the Casa Hogar, along with Juan Carlos, which was a great honour and equally ironic at the same time.

By the time we had had a couple of beers and made our proposals, it was getting quite late. I had a palta sandwich and a shot of rum to warm me when we got back home. I noticed that I was actually getting quite good at balancing on my shoes in the cold of night before I climbed into bed at around midnight. It was freezing that night and the dogs were restless, my twelve blankets were quite some comfort.

Thursday 1ˢᵗ October

I got up slightly late, at around 8.30 a.m. and had a wash and breakfast, accompanied by the chickens, dogs, cats, kittens and cows. It was another beautiful, bright sunshiny day high in the Andes, in the village of Apuquri.

Marie Paz and I got down to the building site with the dogs at around 10.00 a.m. The men had again split into two teams of three. One to finish the adobe by filling in between the roof joists and building up the gable ends and the other to finish the cutting and the nailing of the roof battens in situ. I have a sneaking suspicion that they would have worked in one team given half a chance, I think Marie Paz must have had another word on the QT.

I spent most of my time that morning carrying adobe bricks to build up the gable ends and generally helping out, including cutting and nailing some of battens. It was a normal day at work, and again a pleasure to be working outside in the fresh air, far from the madding crowd of the technological world of the 21ˢᵗ Century.

I got back to work late after lunch at around 2.30 p.m. I had had to have a short nap, the lack of oxygen in the air still had its effect on occasion and I needed to sleep, if only for a few minutes. Until the red haemoglobin levels have increased sufficiently the heart has to work harder than normal to compensate for the low oxygen density in the air. These red corpuscles soak up oxygen like sponges, and may be part of the secret of the longevity of the mountain people.

Even after almost a month at altitude, I could still become quite drowsy sometimes.

Juan Carlos arrived at 3.30 p.m. with tableos, whatever they may be, probably nothing, nothing apparently. He didn't do any work on site, but he did have a chat. Juan Carlos did not appear to do very much, except when he left with Roger at 5.30 p.m., when he did spend some time cutting the pig carcasses into pieces; half of which were to be carried and stored at his place, in the municipal building, for the following evening. The other half of the meat stayed where it was, hanging in the house nearby, to be brought to the faena on Saturday.

We did eventually get our double gas hob back that day, Juan Carlos had brought it around on his way to work; which was something of a relief because it meant that Marie Paz didn't have to make a fire every night to cook on, and I didn't have to carry any more leño up the steep incline with Hercules.

It also turned out that the authorities had requested that the Wasi Wasi (literally meaning "house house", however in this case meaning "The roof completion ceremony") was to take place on Monday, because there were two other celebrations elsewhere on Saturday. This meant that the numbers that might turn up at our Wasi Wasi would be vastly depleted if we were to have it on Saturday. In turn this meant that we would have much less help to carry the tiles down from the top of the slope to load out the ridges, to complete the construction of the roof.

I finally arrived home at around 8.00 p.m., having, mainly observed the division of one of the carcasses in preparation for our celebration the following evening. Marie Paz and I had a light supper of soup, and then shared a couple of glasses of rum before we retired for the night. The dogs were quite vociferous and there was a chill in the air when I finally floated off to sleep.

Friday 2nd October

I awoke with a very bad stomach, which meant that we didn't get to work until 10.00 a.m., following a wash in the morning sun in the garden and a sumptuous breakfast, of course.

I met Oscar at the top of the slope when I arrived at work; he was working with Don Moreno. He told me that his wife had recently gone to hospital with appendicitis. She was about to begin her second week in hospital and he missed her, very much; his eyes were full of sadness, especially as he had been to see her in Hospital the night before. He could not afford to go to Abancay every night, which did not help matters, which added to his discomfort, but she was being well cared for. He was entirely open in his distress; there was no reason for him to do otherwise, he didn't have a stiff upper lip.

Juan Carlos arrived mid-morning and it wasn't long before Marie Paz had left with him to go downtown to buy some things for the fiesta such as papas, condiments and a couple of bottles of flavoured rum to accompany the usual chicha and cañazo.

When they had gone I spent the morning working with Roger and Don Fernando loading out and laying adobe bricks between the roof joists. I walked up the steep incline with Hercules to lunch alone. I had finished my solitary meal, of a warmed up bowl of soup and bread rolls, by the time Marie Paz and Juan Carlos returned from Chalhuanca. I have to say, that I might have suffered a pang of envy, which is not an emotion I often feel.

I was working again by around 2.00 p.m., where I continued loading out adobe bricks until the job was done, the in fills between the joists and the gables had to be completed prior to the faena, and otherwise we wouldn't be able put the tiles on the roof. We managed to complete the job early that afternoon with Roger and Don Fernando laying the bricks, Constantino mixing the muck and Hercules loading it out, from a heavy plastic bucket, which he carried on his shoulder as usual.

We finished at around 4.00 p.m. when Hercules and I gathered together two great big bundles of leña and took them to Marie Paz who was preparing the fire to cook the chancho (pig) at the village hall. Hercules and I then walked the streets of Apuquri to various houses of friends and cousins to find a hoya and a parole, which are heavy duty iron cooking utensils, Peruvian style. It turned out that they simply don't have enough wood in Apuquri to burn to spit roast a pig, in fact despite their promise, that was never the intention. An abundance of fire wood is something which we take for granted in the UK, but there aren't so many trees in that part of the Apurimac region where Apuquri sits.

Eventually we managed to find both a parole and a hoya after being directed through several streets to several different houses, which took us on a very pleasant scenic route around the village back up to the hall. When the delivery was complete we returned to work as everyone was clearing up, and we all started drinking shots of rum mixed with shots of coke, from one glass, with a little help from Pachamama. Then some of the men went home to change, but Hercules and I walked back up to meet Juan Carlos and Marie Paz who was getting the food ready with a friend, ready to put the pork in a hoya and a parole, to fry it slowly over the fire close to a wall of the building under an adjacent archway.

We helped out with whatever needed to be done with drinks in our hands. We collected wood and I found some kindling to start the fire which we had made under the archway, close to the wall, in the hope that it wouldn't burn down.

Before the festivities were fully underway, it was time to settle the account so I asked Juan Carlos for a refund of my expenses. I had paid Sol. 208.00 on various things, and I didn't really mind not getting it all back but Juan Carlos only paid me Sol. 98.00; he said that the Sol. 30 for the beer was my expense, yet I had had to pay it because Juan Carlos hadn't been there to buy the customary drink in return for the gift of the pigs. He also said Sol. 60 for a taxi of Sol. 40 and Sol. 20 were trips that weren't necessary, which was slightly incongruous, due to the fact that if Marie Paz and I hadn't gone to town we would have had no hammers or nails to build the roof. As "Padrino" I also had to pay Sol. 20 towards the crosses that were to be put into the ridge along the top of the roof of the Casa Hogar. It didn't really matter, it was a charity after all, but there most certainly was a discrepancy in the calculations of the accounting department.

Still, as the evening progressed, a few people began to arrive and we all stood around drinking, as is the wont of any party. Juan's brother turned up, looking quite Italian, he arrived with a few others that I hadn't seen before. It became a very pleasant evening, in and around the municipal hall, just standing around talking about nothing in particular, exchanging pleasantries, much in the same manner as any small party anywhere else in the world.

Whilst we were taking our first drinks we were each provided with a plate of rice, potatoes and probably the most organic pork that I have ever eaten, or ever will, in my entire life. The food was excellent, incredibly tasty and entirely natural, slightly dark succulent, richly flavoured pork that melted in the mouth. Juan Carlos told me that he had heard the sound of a Puma growling by the window the night before, a Puma that had smelled the meat in the room, not so far from the window sill.

When the drinks were in full flow, I felt quite challenged when Don Ignacio made a point of asking me quite directly why I was there working in Apuquri. I merely told them that I strongly believed that if you help others it will improve your own life, and that it was an invaluable experience for me to spend some time living so far away from England, in a place where I could improve my Spanish. They seemed satisfied with this explanation and I was somewhat relieved when they actually applauded their approval of my support for the project.

It didn't take long to tidy up and the women mostly did that, which meant that there wasn't a lot to be done when the time came to go home. Marie Paz and I didn't stay up too long, we were tired and there was work to be done the following day.

Saturday 3rd October

I got up at 8.20 a.m. and waited for Gilberto, whoever he may have been, as instructed. I think he was a friend of Marie Paz's; he was going to bring some food of some kind to the Wasi Wasi. This meant that I had some time to kill so I read up on some Peruvian history.

I discovered that apparently war was often created by poor interpreters and translators in the time of the Conquistadores. Two Peruvians were taken to Spain in that epoch for three months to learn Spanish, but this was not long enough to learn an entire language and many mistakes were made in consequence. Deliberate or otherwise, the confusion that arose was enough to exacerbate conflict between the Spanish invaders and the indigenous people. It seemed that the history written by Europeans about barbaric South American Indians was becoming less and less reliable.

Gilberto finally arrived sometime after 10.00 a.m. with some provisions for the Faena. He was an amenable young man of around 30 years of age, who had the dark complexion that was common to the region. By the time we had collected our things together we eventually arrived at the Faena at the building site at around 11.00 a.m.

When we arrived Marie Paz informed us that it would have been infinitely better for us to have waited until Monday for the Faena, as only around fifteen people turned up at first, as predicted. The sparse population of volunteers had been spread over three fiestas on the same day. The reason why we hadn't waited until Monday was of course because Juan Carlos had wanted to get back to Lima sooner rather than later, which I'm afraid was most inconsiderate, he could have waited a couple of days.

However fortunately for us, as time went by, more people turned up and we began to make chains of people, mainly consisting of women and children, to pass the terracotta roof tiles down to the building works, from the stacks at the top of the slope. Then at the end of the chain, our team were laying the tiles on the roof. It was a sort of Peruvian version of an Amish building festival, the main difference being that we were constantly supplied with chicha, cañazo, and beer throughout the day by little old ladies walking around wearing many skirts and fedoras. The same ladies also cooked the rest of the chancho, which was done on an open fire made on the ground close to the building itself. The chancho was of course delicious, presented with papas and rice in a piquant sauce, with a garnish of locally grown herbs.

I was Padrino which meant that as the roof took shape, I had to climb up into the rafters at the centre of the roof and place a decorative cross on the top of the ridge, the same cross that can be seen on all houses in rural Peru, placed to bless the house. This particular Casa Hogar had two crosses and two Padrinos, as mentioned, myself and Juan Carlos, for all the wonderful work we had done.

There was a direct relationship between the time when our friend wanted to return to Lima and the number people at the Wasi Wasi. If he had left on Saturday a few people would have come, if he had left on Sunday a few more people would have come and if he had left on Monday a few more than before would have come. Was this relationship inversely proportional? I like to think so. The longer Juan

Carlos stayed the more people would help, that is until the optimum Tuesday. It certainly wasn't optimum Saturday. The more people at the Wasi Wasi, the more work would be done and the better for the community, but that did not appear to concern Juan Carlos, he just didn't care.

Juan Carlos had been absent for far too much time, he had left Marie Paz and I to do his job, he had spent charity money entertaining himself and his girlfriend, he had taken the side of the miners and now to end it all as a final gesture he had had the Wasi Wasi at the most inconvenient time for the community. Ironically he could have been honoured as an absentee Padrino, he could have left us to have the fiesta on Monday without his attendance, after he had gone.

Nonetheless the festivities continued, I bought a case of beer as did Juan Carlos, which was par for the course as Padrino.

Despite any shortcomings, the day, in actual fact worked out very well. We moved hundreds of tiles and the roof was almost finished by the time the people stopped work and we gathered in the Casa Hogar for the Faenees to dance the night away.

Juan Carlos couldn't stay, even on the most inconvenient day at he left for Lima at around 7.30 p.m. Marie Paz and I took flight, not much later, at 8.30 that night. She treated my arm with the wonder potion, and she made up a bottle of the stuff for me to take away with me, whilst we had a glass of rum and finished our packing.

It was my last evening in Apuquri and the next day I was leaving to go to Lima. I knew that I would be free from any threat, so as a passing gesture I wrote a contract for Marie Paz, in Spanish. It seemed to me that it was potentially too dangerous to have written it earlier. I wrote it to help her, in order that she may attempt to negotiate on behalf of the community, to prevent the exploitation of the campesinos. I knew that there was great potential for skulduggery on the part of the miners, so, inter alia, I inserted a clause that the miners should pay the legal fees for the community in the event of contractual dispute. I didn't think the miners would notice such a thing. I also inserted a condition that the environment would be left untainted and a clause that everything would be left in apple pie order. I also gave the villagers a percentage of the profits, in that any funds received would be held in trust to be managed by a committee for the benefit of the community. I knew that without that, any income would have even greater potential to harm what was a very pleasant place to live. To what extent it would have been acted upon would of course have been left open to question nonetheless, but I did have faith in Marie Paz.

We finally retired to bed at around 10.00 p.m., tired and exhausted by the day's events. It was my last night under my twelve blankets, listening to the dogs in the still of night, fending off the sand flies, if only I could see them. No more freezing cold, no more choking myself awake at night. Goodnight Apu San Francisco.

Sunday 4th October

I slept, unusually, right through that night, uninterrupted until 7.00 a.m. After I got up and got dressed, I walked into the dining room from my bedroom, half awake, when I had to chase a couple of boiled egg eating chickens from the table; so I promptly went across the road and bought three more, from our local store. Whilst I ate breakfast of porridge and milk, with boiled eggs and bread, Marie Paz washed a few clothes for me and hung them up in the garden, in the hope that they would dry by the time we got back from our morning excursion, on that bright, bright, bright, sunshiny day.

We were to walk up the mountain path to meet Don Prudencia, he had invited me to visit, whilst his clique worked in the cákras. This one in particular, was on some of the highest cultivable slopes, not far beneath the final rocky inclines of the mountain peaks that stood majestic all around us.

We walked down to the town square and took the low road towards the path that led up to Puka Wasi, high up on the slopes above. On the way of out towards the outskirts, some of Marie Paz's friends waved to us, as we walked on by, they were building a concrete framed house, just on the edge of town. One of the more senior ladies invited us in for a drink, to join in the celebration, which we had to accept to avoid offence; it was shortly after 10 o'clock in the morning.

We walked into the Sunday morning building site which was merely the empty concrete framework of a house, where

I was introduced to the two young men. Roberto and Eduardo were responsible for the construction of the two storey building that we stood in, they were in their early twenties and in an excellent mood. I had never met them before, but they seemed to know me. They were building a house for Roberto because he was about to get married and needed a home for his family. They had no idea what a mortgage was, the house would be built by their friends.

Probably a significant part of the reason why they were grinning so much was because they were absolutely plastered; they had red rings around their distant smiling eyes and insisted that we had some whisky. One of the little old ladies handed me a ¾ pint glass, which she proceeded to fill with pink chicha, which Marie Paz reliably informed that I had to neck in one. Then I was offered a shot of the local dark brown cañazo, which they called whiskey, which, again, I had to neck in one, which I did, and then I was offered another which again, I had to neck in one, which I did, which pleased everyone, they were so very warm and welcoming.

I was surprised that they had even heard of me, but they were very respectful, they treated me like an old friend, which may have been for my support for the Casa Hogar. The mountain people may own very little, and they may seem to be uneducated in a University sense, but they are incredibly civilized. After a very brief exchange of pleasantries and our first drinks of the day, Marie Paz and I said our farewells, as time, was beginning to slip away.

We wended our way out of the village up the well-worn trail, towards Puka Wasi, up along beside the narrow stream that followed the vale. The path slipped between the cákras that filled the slopes around us. There was a clear blue, sun filled sky above us with hardly a cloud in sight. As we left the metropolis below us, a peaceful serenity descended all around, we could have been walking through a film set, we could have been in a scene from a book. While we walked up the mountain path through the idyllic countryside, we met the mayor's right hand man, coming down the hill on horseback. He was wearing the traditional garb of a brightly patterned poncho, and a large brimmed sandy coloured hat; from beneath which he looked at us through his red rimmed eyes. He greeted us with gleaming white teeth, in the most genteel manner, as he rocked down past us, on the back of his sure footed steed.

We continued on our hike and saw another group of men and women working in the fields, a few hundred meters away over to the left. Marie Paz called over to them, to ask where we might find the cákra of Don Prudencia; they shouted to us, they didn't know exactly where the cákra in question was, but they thought it was further up the pathway, we waved goodbye as we continued up towards the higher slopes.

A few minutes later we saw another group to our left, working a steep sloped cákra with a pair of Toros Bravos with a wooden yoke lashed across their shoulders. They were pulling a plough, gently persuaded by Antonio. A stout broad shouldered man who I had met on the first day with Juan Carlos, when he was making adobe bricks with his friends and covered in mud, and today was no exception. They called him Toro, because he was strong, or rather he wasn't. Marie Paz called out to them and asked for directions to Don Prudencia's cákra once more, but this time they called us over, and insisted that we join them for a drink.

We took a detour of one hundred meters or so from the path, through what was an idyllic setting. The cákra smelt of the freshly turned earth. As it was being churned by the bulls, a young woman followed along behind throwing seeds of maize into the earth, from a rolled up shawl wrapped around her waist. A group of woman were sitting under a group of trees, in the shade as the sun glittered through the leaves, at the foot of the descent of the cákra. They were incredibly warm in their welcome; we were greeted with another large glass of chicha, which of course I had to drink as though I were suffering from a terrible thirst, while making sure that I saluted Pachamama by pouring the first and last drops to the ground; it had its effect, the maize alcohol made for a clear untroubled view of the world. Marie Paz joined me in a drink when, Antonio, his broad face smiling, his perfect teeth shining, and his big dark eyes gleaming from the pleasure of his work, offered me a long heavy stick to direct the bulls to plough the field. I was honoured to be given such a task, and it was not difficult, but strenuous, following the bulls and making sure they didn't stray from the line of the furrows. The ground was rough and the incline was steep, which took its toll on my unaccustomed legs, but it was pleasure to work up there in the untainted world of the campesinos. After about a quarter of an hour, and a few passes, Antonio decided that I had done enough and the ladies decided I should have another large cup of chicha.

We went on our way and waved good bye as we continued up the path, we still didn't know where we would find the cákra of Don Prudencia. It was by then 11.30 in the morning and we were only half way up the side of the mountain. I had already drunk four large glasses of chicha and at least four big shots of the local cañazo, life wasn't so bad working in the cákras.

As the incline grew steeper, we pulled off the path, to let a young man with a long stick pass, he was promptly followed in quick succession by four rather large Toros Bravos, endowed with incredibly large, ominous looking horns, with a second young man in hot pursuit, brandishing an equally large stick, firmly persuading the huge beasts with a gracious bon viveur, neither man nor beast seemed to have a care in the world. We were lucky to have met them where we did; otherwise we might well have been trampled underfoot, as though we were nothing more than a minor interruption.

When the bulls had passed by we stepped back down onto the path and walked up to the right of the ravine, moving away from Puka Wasi situated high up the slopes to the left. It was there that we came upon an ancient stone wall, which had various forms of vegetation, growing out of it, as it followed the line of the path. It became apparent that the most likely place to find the elusive cákra, was to cross the seemingly insurmountable stone barrier, when as luck would have it; we came upon a break in the barricade.

There opened up in front of us a broad open expanse of cákra where the slope was far less pronounced. A few hundred meters away up the slope were about fifteen men, women and children sitting in small groups, whilst several pairs of men were directing five pairs of Toros Bravos as they ploughed the great cákra in unison; a young woman followed each plough throwing seeds of maize into the newly formed furrows.

One group called us over where Marie Paz introduced me. I found myself talking to two pretty young women, as normal wearing fedoras and many skirts, one of whom was holding her pet lamb in her arms. Victor was also there, coaxing a pair of bulls, but he didn't really speak to us; there was no sign of Don Prudencia, we were in Peru after all.

The ladies offered more chicha, and a couple of shots of cañazo. I had to throw the obligatory drop on the ground at the beginning and end of each glass as a salute to Pachamama and Pachamama. I also had to blow on a bag of maize, when they said something in Quechua, in order that we may be blessed with a good harvest. I was also given a plate of pasta and herbs, served in a broth. Highly nutritious, and very filling, in fact it was too much, especially after so much chicha, which of course I had to drink again.

To sew the maize in the cákras the people in Apuquri get up early in the morning and have a substantial organic breakfast. Full of good food, they then go on a hike with a few, potentially dangerous, majestic bulls, up an archaeologically important Inca trail, high into the second highest mountain range in the world. When they arrive at their designated cákra, they bind the bulls into pairs with old wooden yokes across their necks; to plough the fields walking behind the mighty beasts, where there are no fumes at all. The work is fabulous for the upper body, the legs, the lungs and the cardiovascular system; especially because the air is so thin, where there are absolutely no pollutants at all; this is a workout that you couldn't better with a personal trainer, and in one of the most beautiful places in the world.

At the end of the morning, a piping hot organic picnic lunch is provided, to be enjoyed with all with your family and friends, and then the afternoon is spent back at work. To top it off, during the time of the sembra, many workers spend the working day getting loaded on chicha and cañazo.

There was another slight twist to the time of the sembras. When the work is done, at the end of the day, "La Chicha es buena para la prostata", and the moon had begun to wane, then was the perfect time to sew the seed, and not only for the production of maize. It was not surprising really then, that everyone was in such a good mood whilst they were sowing the cákras, all was not entirely as it may have seemed.

* * *

By the time our lunch was over, I was looking at the world through a contented chicha and cañazo fuelled haze when Marie Paz and I took a different route down the mountainside as we made our way back down the incline into the village. We climbed over another grey stone wall at the back end of the cákra, and found ourselves looking upon descending slopes, so steep that we sometimes had to slide down, interspersed with scrub, that we had to walk around, which took us to another stony mountain trail, that gradually levelled out, into a hillside path that would lead us back into the upper reaches of Apuquri.

Along the way we came across a lair dug out into the hillside set back from the path hidden behind a few bushes. Marie Paz reliably informed me that it had been made by a Puma, which she said were quite common in the area and there were stories of them coming into the village. Pumas were known to have taken children from the village on rare occasion in the past, but Marie Paz said that was not something that particularly worried the locals. The reason was that a Puma will take its quarry away to somewhere safe and hidden, to kill and eat it. If a Puma were to take a child, the child would scream very loudly. When this had happened in the past, the villagers had chased a Puma that couldn't run too quickly due to the weight of the a baby in its mouth; the screams of the infant and the multitude of people in pursuit had frightened the cat into dropping the youngster and running away in fear for its life. Of the event that Marie Paz knew of, fortunately the child had only suffered a few minor cuts and bruises; apparently nothing, nothing apparently.

The descent levelled out as we walked down the mountain path that led us to the street where we arrived at Marie Paz's house, at around 3.00 p.m. We promptly packed my bags, with the clothes that Marie Paz had hung out to dry that morning. I felt a wistful melancholy as we took my few belongings and walked directly into town to look for a taxi. The vacuous tranquillity of the town portrayed an almost eidolic emptiness within the streets; the desolation was perhaps because everyone was working in the cákras.

We found the same open pick-up truck with a metal cage frame over the bed at the back; it was the same truck that had taken us to Puka Wasi for the elections. We climbed into the back where we sat with a couple of men, a woman and a few small children. It was a stupendous way to travel, in the back of a bumpy old pick-up truck in the clear fresh air and the glorious sunshine. I thoroughly enjoyed the hour long drive down the bolder strewn Andean mountain track that led to the road to Chalhuanca, but there was a tinge of sadness in the air. I was going to miss the calm of living so far away from the madness of the 21st century, so far away from such wonderful people. Marie Paz had taught me so much.

* * *

In Cuzco in 1589, one of the last survivors of the original conquerors of Peru wrote in the preamble to his will, inter alia:

"We found these kingdoms in such good order, and the said Incas governed them in such a wise manner that throughout them there was not a thief, nor a vicious man, nor an adulteress, nor was there a bad woman admitted among them, nor were there immoral people. The men had honest and useful occupations. The lands, forests, mines, pastures, houses and all kinds of products were regulated and distributed in such sort that each one knew his property without any other person seizing it or occupying it, nor were there any law suits respecting it...... the motive which obliges me to make this statement is the discharge of my conscience, as I find myself guilty. For we have destroyed by our evil example, the people who had such government as was enjoyed by these natives. They were so free from the committal of crimes or excesses, as well men and women, that the Indian who had 100,000 pesos worth of gold or silver in his house, left it open merely placing a small stick against the door, as a sign that its master was out. With that, according to their custom, no one could enter or take anything that was there. When they saw that we put locks and keys on our doors, they supposed that it was for fear of them, that they might not kill us, but not because they believed that anyone would steal the property of another. So that when they found that we had thieves among us, and men who sought to make their daughters commit sin, they despised us."

Don Mancio Serre Leguisarno

Epilogue

It is said that the Incas were expecting the Spanish; they had predicted their arrival in 1526 and ironically, the subsequent demise of their own civilisation. When the Spanish set foot on the shores of the town which is now known as Tumbes, on the North West coast of a country which is now known as Peru, they were welcomed by the indigenous people with open arms, and the sight of the gold and silver jewellery that adorned some of those people, excited the blood of the Spanish. The vision reinforced their resolve to return in search of the riches of the legendary golden city of El Dorado that they believed was hidden in the depths of South America, and in a sense they found it.

European Historians write that the Inca Empire began from around 1410 a.d. but this is not certain by any means. The Inca tribe emanated from Cuzco situated high in the Andes in South Central Peru; they managed to dominate most of Western South America to create the one of the largest empires known to man at that time, no mean feat by any means. By the time the Spanish had arrived, the Incas had successfully conquered an area that stretched from the frontiers of the Chilean desert in the South, to the jungles of Colombia in the North, from the Pacific coast to the West, to the Amazon jungle in the East.

As is normal with any powerful regime, the Incas demanded taxation from the many tribes that they had subjugated, which was generally not popular amongst the local people, despite the benefit of the social security that the tariff provided. The tax wasn't exorbitant; it consisted of about 65 days labour a year, from every able man and woman, in support of the state. The populous were put to work in the terraced lands of the Andes where they built a network of tall, ventilated stone towers that were filled with dried maize or dried potatoes. The dried crops were set on a bed of thyme at least a metre in height within the base of the stone columns; the airflow of the aroma, created from strategically placed holes at the base of the walls, kept the pests away from the food in storage. This configuration meant that the entire community could be fed, in the event that the harvest failed, for up to three years. It was a system that displayed many socialist ideologies aside from the inherent tiers of class structure clearly designed to maintain a functional system of control. In reality the Inca governance was far more humane than that of the subsequent Spanish administration that was to impose its will from 1536, when the Spanish finally conquered the Inca Empire.

In 1532 Pizarro and his motley crew of 158 Conquistadores, returned to the bay of San Mateo, not far north of Tumbes on the North West coast of what is now Peru. They were fortunate to arrive at a time when the Inca Empire had been weakened by a civil war between two half-brothers who were the Inca kings, Atahualpa and Huasca. Armed with information gleaned from the local leaders, the Spanish travelled south inland across the mountains to a town called Cajamarca in search of Atahualpa, who was residing there with his armies, having killed his brother Huasca, he had become the Ruler of the Inca Empire.

When the Spanish arrived at Cajamarca the odds were stacked against them; they were outnumbered considerably, but they did have some advantage. It is believed that almost all of the proletariat Incas held the Spanish in awe; as they thought that they may have been Gods. The illusion of men on horseback to the impressionable Inca masses was one of four legged beings; this misapprehension was further substantiated by the Spanish use of firepower from cannon and muskets, never before seen by the indigenous tribesmen.

Pizarro had found himself in what some may describe as a difficult situation. He knew that it would be suicide to attempt open warfare. Atahualpa's army numbered over 80,000 troops and understandably did not feel threatened by the foreign force numbering only 158 men with 62 horses. The reports from Atahualpa's spies confirm that though his men may have been uncertain as to whether the Spanish were deities, Atahualpa had no such misapprehension. He had planned to recruit some of the Conquistadores into his own service and to capture the Spanish firearms and horses for use in his own armies; then he was planning to kill the rest of the force of 158 at his leisure. The Spanish had no idea of Atahualpa's plan and invited the Emperor into Cajamarca, who gracefully accepted. Atahualpa marched slowly down the hill towards the city, and then ordered the majority of his army of 80,000 to camp outside the city walls. Atahualpa was so secure in his position of power that, as a gesture of amity and absolute confidence, he entered the city with his unarmed retinue of 6,000, unopposed.

When the entourage entered the town square on the evening of 16 November 1532, Friar Vincente de Valverde approached the Inca leader and ordered him to accept Catholicism as his faith and to accept Charles V, the Holy Roman Emperor,[lxxxiv] as his sovereign. With no intention of acceding to the Spaniard's demands, insulted and mildly confused, Atahualpa did politely enquire as to the Spaniard's faith and king. Though it is not entirely clear as to what exactly happened next, the hidden Spanish troops were exhorted to attack in the name of the Catholic Church, which apparently absolved them of divine retribution for the forthcoming murderous assault on the apparently over confident Inca assembly.

At the signal of attack the Spanish unleashed gunfire upon the almost defenceless Incan entourage in such a determined action that it had a devastating effect. The Spanish used four canons in combination with fusillade of gunfire. The Inca had never experienced such firepower before; the Spanish utilised their 62 horsemen in a cavalry charge, the Incas had never seen horses before; the Spanish also had steel swords, helmets and armour; the Incas wore leather body armour and were unarmed. It is said that during the massacre at Cajamarca the natives were so terrified that they were climbing over each other in a panicked attempt to escape the wrath of the Spanish armoury. Within the space of just a few hours, though many had been trampled to death, the Spanish had killed or wounded between five and six thousand unarmed men, without the loss of one single Spanish life; that meant each Conquistador had killed an average of over 35 almost defenceless men before they decided to stop the bloodbath and the massacre was ended. It is easy to see why cricket never quite caught on in Spain.

Once the Spanish had captured Atahualpa and his top commanders, the Incan forces rapidly became disorganised, they had in effect been decapitated. Pizarro had put himself in control and demanded that Atahualpa order that a room be filled with gold and silver as a ransom for his own release. Gold and silver did not have the same value to the Inca population as it did elsewhere; to the Incas these abundant precious metals had no real, intrinsic value in the European sense.

Under a certain amount of duress, basically death or gold and silver, Atahualpa sent orders throughout his kingdom to bring gold and silver to Cajamarca. After some time the elected room was eventually filled with what is said to have been 24 tons of gold and silver. When the room was full, and Pizarro had got what he asked for, he went back on his word; he ordered that the Emperor be garrotted, probably under the excuse that the Emperor would not denounce his gods and become a Catholic. However before he was killed, it is said that Pizarro asked the Great Inca where he was to find the lost city of El Dorado. Atualpa told him it was in a remote region in the Northern Amazonas, which is why the city now known as a Chachapoyas, was built, a few years later on 5 September 1538, as a staging post to search for gold.

Sadly the vast majority of the precious metal that filled the room, was melted down and the Inca artwork was lost forever.[lxxxv] The ingots were transported back to Spain. I can imagine the British keeping the spoils. Though I would like to think in those circumstances they would have kept their word, but who will ever know? Perceived integrity was after all the backbone of the British Empire, I say, quite different to that of the Spanish; which ironically was also the conceived opinion of Simon Bolivar, as quoted beneath his strategically placed statue in Belgravia.

* * *

Following the massacre of Cajamarca, the Conquistadores began their 400 mile journey further south across the Andes en route to the city of Cuzco, the heart of the Inca Empire. Their greed drove them on to search for even greater riches, in their quest to discover the legendary city of gold "El Dorado".

The Spanish were faced with a seemingly impossible task but they did have a certain amount of good fortune; for example a few of the indigenous tribes were not entirely enamoured with their Inca rulers.

When they arrived in the Northern Amazonas the Spanish came upon the Chupapoyas, probably the happiest tribe on the planet; who were a group who had conveniently been at war with the Incas for possibly as many as sixty years prior to their final domination in or around 1470 a.d.. This meant that the Spanish Conquistadores were able to form an allegiance with the Chupapoyas in their campaign to conquer the Inca Empire; which they did with the greatest of ease.

Later en camino the Spanish passed through what is now known as the Montaro valley where the Huanca[lxxxvi] people live to this day, in the Junin region of Central Peru. It is not clear how they were able to form an alliance with the Huancas, but they did so, probably along the lines of "no taxation without representation".

Further South en camino the Spanish managed to enlist the help of another tribe, known as the Chancas, who then lived and still live to this day, in and around the Apurimac region of South Central Peru. The Chancas had never acceded to the domination of the Incas; agreement to co-exist had only ever been established by treaty.

These allegiances were invaluable to the Spanish Conquistadores; it has become apparent that without the help of the Huancas, the Chancas, and the Chupapoyas, it is doubtful whether the Spanish would ever have achieved what that they did. In fact it would not be unreasonable to suggest that the greater part of the success of the Spanish conquest of South America in the 16th Century was down to a bunch of Huancas and the subsequent economic development of the World. Not a lot of people know that.

* * *

Another most severe Inca misfortune assisted the Spanish in the devastation of the Inca Empire. For the most part, the native Inca population had little or no resistance to the European influenza brought to South America by the Spaniards. They had never been exposed to what is normally regarded as a mild inconvenience to those accustomed to it, and in consequence an epidemic arose; in effect the common cold eventually killed about three quarters of the indigenous Inca population, which is said to have numbered approximately 5,000,000. It is also apparent that over eighty percent of other indigenous populations, Los Ribereños, who lived along the edge of the rivers of the Amazonas, also disappeared in consequence of the same disease, due to the arrival of the Spanish explorer Francisco de Orellana and his crew in 1541. Their population may also have numbered in excess of 5,000,000, according to recent archaeological discoveries, but that is another story.

Those who survived, suffered under Spanish rule, during the many years that followed the eventual Spanish domination of the Inca Empire in 1536. Countless numbers of the indigenous people were put to work in gold and silver mines where life expectancy was not the best; they were used, in effect, as slaves to extract the gold and silver deposits. The work was and is to this day, extremely dangerous and so unhealthy that it has shortened the labourers' lives considerably. The Spanish extraction of precious metals in South America has not only harmed many communities, it has also caused some not inconsiderable environmental damage.

The mines are still in operation today.

* * *

The Spanish minted gold and silver coins in the Americas, known as Doubloons and Escudos respectively, from the late 15th century to the end of the 19th century. These coins became so successful that they were circulated throughout most of the world by the late 19th century, to the extent that they were in reality, the legal currency of the United States until 1857.

The silver Spanish dollar coin was worth eight Reales and could be physically cut into eight pieces, or "bits", to make the money more easily manageable — hence the colloquial name "pieces of eight" commonly used by parrots in pirate films. The dollar coin could also be cut into quarters, and two pieces of eight or "two bits" became American slang for a quarter dollar, or 25 cents. That slang is still in use in the good ol' U.S.of A today. The American dollar, probably the most widely used currency in the world throughout and since the industrial revolution, is based on the Spanish Escudo. It seems that South American gold and silver is the origin of modern western legal tender; it also provided the finance that was the mainstay, which enabled Spain to create an empire, upon which the sun never set. In actual fact the result is that the currency made from Inca gold and silver led us to the commercial world in which we live today.

Footnotes

i   Good day Sir, I am pleased to make your acquaintance.

ii   A French phrase probably brought over the Channel at around 1066.

iii   Apuquri turned out to rest at around 3,700 m above sea level.

iv   Drug Traffickers.

v   Another French expression, that William the Conqueror has a lot to answer for.

vi   At the time, of over £1,000.00 each.

vii   Apu means spirit in Quechua, Apurimac means "The spirit that speaks". This is because in the rainy season during the European time of winter, thunder rolls across the mountains of the valley, every day at around 4.30 p.m., before the onset of a torrential thunderstorm. When you are there, it is as though the spirits of the mountains are talking to the people.

viii   Quechua for depth or valley.

ix   The Spirit of San Francisco.

x   The Spirit that Snores.

xi   In fact walking around in mud will stimulate the pressure points on the bottom the feet, which will stimulate the release of hormones that will create the pleasant feeling of a natural high.

xii   A remnant of Spanish Colonialism. The occasional animal was found in the bullring, having been discovered wandering the streets. For release a fine of Sol. 5 was due for small animals and Sol. 10 was due for large animals.

xiii   Mother earth.

xiv   Mother earth again. Father Sun, AKA Tayta Inti, didn't get a look in.

xv   For all you North Americans out there, plastered means drunk in this context. It doesn't mean getting covered in plaster, which may be fun, but would also be quite ridiculous.

xvi   Rural people, not effete gay people.

xvii   Sadly I later discovered that that was not entirely the case. Piquipiqui (Quechua) on occasion are a problem and are eradicated by insecticide.

xviii   Literally "House home" in this case meaning "Dormitory shelter".

xix   I later discovered that Cabo had sired many a sibling.

xx   Muck in England is a colloquial term for "wet cement".

xxi   Toros Bravos, in fact a remnant of the Spanish Empire.

xxii   Chicha is an ancient concoction made from maize fermented with various herbs. It lasts up to four days in warmer climes, and up to ten in the mountains. The alcohol level increases up until it becomes undrinkable. At later stages it is likened to a very strong spirit that may be used in cooking. This maize beer produces a mild euphoric high which is not the same as that produced from alcohol made from wheat, grapes or hops. When it is ready to be sold, a white cloth is hung outside the off license, (In Bolivia the colour of the cloth is red) in much the same way as a sign was originally only hung outside a pub in England, when the beer was ready to be drunk.

xxiii   A white rum made locally, so strong on occasion, that it could burn a hole in the carpet if there were one.

xxiv   Meaning drunk in English, not angry as in North American.

xxv   Ibid.

xxvi   The Mayor.

xxvii   Known locally as *"Razon Social"*.

xxviii   The sowing of seeds.

xxix   I later learned that women in Peru did not gain a right to an education, and that right was not often accepted until 1975 and thereafter. Women were not allowed to become Pilots, Architects or members of the Police Force until the 1980's. Cleo Fé for example, could not read or write and numbers were also a problem for her. When Cleo Fé sold a cow, Marie Paz had to count the money for her. She also had to make her funeral preparations. Cleo Fé wants to be dressed in white of course, in a polished beige coloured coffin. Cleo Fé had ten children. Sadly one died at six years of age and another at twelve, she brought up four boys and four girls.

Marie Paz's mother cannot read or write either.

The simple act of counting in the more developed World is taken for granted. In South America there are many who suffer from a lack of an education which goes unnoticed throughout most of the first world.

xxx   Campesino.

xxxi   But only in terms of money.

xxxii   Meaning "Jumper" or "One that jumps".

xxxiii   Or "colectivo".

xxxiv   Metaphorically speaking of course, it is also something that I would not like to envisage.

xxxv   Meaning "Red House" in Quechua.

xxxvi   When asked if the bowl was over 500 years old, Rebecca said it was, but that may have involved some poetic license.

xxxvii   Meaning scissors, in English. Pronounced "tea hare rah"

xxxviii   Guinea Pig is regarded as a delicacy in Peru, Bolivia, Ecuador and other regions of South America.

xxxix   In exactly the same way as the President of the United States of America, El Presidente could not be elected for more than two consecutive terms of office.

xl   AKA on this occasion, paint stripper.

xli   The same standard width of a solid Victorian brick wall.

xlii   I can only imagine he was away with the fairies.

xliii   In Spanish of course. In fact I may not have mentioned that all the dialogue was in Spanish, with perhaps a little Quechua thrown in for good measure.

xliv   Pronounced "Ooh roo roon high". I may have discovered a new species of bee, unknown to the Western World.

xlv   This type of thin yellow straw, called paja, (pronounced "pa-ha"), was mixed with mud for the manufacture of Adobe bricks.

xlvi   Pronounced "Tey ha Andina" with a slightly guttural ha!

xlvii   A word of French Origin, probably introduced by the Normans.

xlviii   That is Norman again.

xlix   Ironically a caña in a Spanish bar in Spain is a small glass of draft beer, a little less than half a pint.

l   As before, meaning "Corrugated iron".

li   Ibid. Insecticide may be used to control an attack of Piquipiqui.

lii   It seems that if earth is left uncultivated in the mountains, a lawn will grow naturally, as in the pathways of Puka Wasi.

liii   A pretentious way of saying "on the way home".

liv   A Faena is an event where people gather together for a common purpose, be it to work, or to celebrate, often both.

lv   Spanish for butcher.

lvi   This word is clearly derived from the Spanish "Casarse" meaning "to be married".

lvii   I have no idea, I didn't understand a word. Anyone?

lviii   One being of certain islands of Lake Titicaca, which is believed to be the place from whence the great God Creator, Viracocha, arose, who must have known a thing or two.

lix   As before, meaning "country people".

lx   Peruvian Chinese fried rice. Delicious.

lxi   I know what this Quechuan word means, but I'm not going to translate.

lxii   Much as Ronald Reagan did, the ex-president of the USA and close ally of Margaret Thatcher. In the 1980's the most powerful world leader, made decisions according to the word of his astrologer.

lxiii   The Valley of the Parrots..... where many parrots lived. Where many pandemoniums, (or companies) of green parrots can be seen.

lxiv   The Hotel of the Parrots..... where many parrots stay when on holiday, I assume.

lxv   Literally translated "coffee with milk".

lxvi   The House.

lxvii   The Beach of San Ignacio.

lxviii Meaning "The second settlement of Basa's people", named after the ancient Saxon tribe of the same name. This Hampshire town was originally the place where livestock were kept, where Basing was the main settlement of the tribe, being "Basa's place". There are other places.

lxix   A German expression, which I hope is self-explanatory.

lxx   Some of which are known to weigh over 100 tons. A few examples can be seen high above the city of Ollantaytumbo. There are other cities.

lxxi   The Maya clearly had a sophisticated written language of which examples exist and there is no reason to suggest that this would not have been parallel to that of the Inca Empire.

lxxii   A cheeky little French number often found at pretentious heights.

lxxiii Another good French red wine, often sadly overlooked, rather fresh and somewhat rustic on occasion.

lxxiv   Ibid.

lxxv   Ibid.

lxxvi   Meaning firewood.

lxxvii Ibid.

lxxviii The ceremonial sowing of maize.

lxxix   Ibid.

lxxx   Hot springs.

lxxxi   Palta is Quechua for Avacado. The word Avocado originates from "ahuácatl" from the Aztec (Mexica) language of Nahuatl, meaning the same as the Greek word for Orchid, which is the name for a particular part of the male anatomy.

lxxxii   That is if there were any in Peru. It is probably less accurate to say "As the condor flies", as they tend to fly in circles.

lxxxiii   A ceremonial killing, normally of a pig, normally in Spain.

lxxxiv   He was also, inter alia, Charles I, the first true King of Spain, and also the Archduke of Austria. In effect Spain was controlled by the Habsburg Empire at the time.

lxxxv   It is said that some of the Gold and Silver ransom was lost en route to Cajamarca and remains to be found in the Northern Amazonas.

lxxxvi   Pronounced "wan-kerr", named after a type of stone, formed in the shape of a pointed obelisk, found in a place known locally as a "Huayco" (or "Quebrada" in Spanish) from which the name of the "Huanca" tribe is derived. The Spanish translation is "Gilipoyas".